Mission Now

Trev Gregory

Authentic
LIFESTYLE

To my family, who allow me to do what I do, and to my friends, who support our lifestyle choice. But particular thanks and dedication to my wife, Denice – mother, friend, thinker and counsellor.

Contents

Part III – Developing A Mission Lifestyle

Preface

Global mission is changing. Or perhaps more accurately the perception of global mission is changing. To some this is good news, to others it is an obvious move, and to others it brings utter panic and insecurity.

To some, mission is for a select minority of fanatical believers from the West going overseas to work long term, full time, in evangelism and church planting. This colonial view is far too narrow and outdated. Mission today is truly global. It involves the church in the east, north, south and west of the globe taking seriously the mission of God. Because we are leaving behind this 'West to the rest' mentality, we can begin to see the truly global nature of the Body of Christ and its impact on the world today.

But the perception of mission is changing not only far beyond our European borders. It is changing within them too. It is changing because not only are we now receiving missionaries from the nations we traditionally sent them to, but because at the heart of the local church perceptions have changed as to the role and mandate of mission agencies and the local church. For the first time in centuries we see Europe, to use the traditional mission agency language, 'as a mission field'. Therefore the focus of mission has become local. Mission is to happen where *I* am.

But this is not all. We have an increasingly global outlook on life. This is bringing about the death of the 'foreign' and 'home' mission ideas, perceptions and practices of the past. Such a simplistic view of mission does not stand up to either mission practice or biblical understanding as we enter the twenty-first century. Mission is local and global.

Some see these changes as an obvious development and do not know what all the fuss is about. If this is you, then this book will help you understand more clearly your thoughts and actions on mission. Hopefully, too, it will go some way in translating the current theory and practice of global mission.

Others see these changes as signalling the decline of mission. I seriously question and doubt this view, and suggest that what we could possibly be witnessing is a resurgence of global mission along biblical lines not witnessed for many centuries, as every believer takes up the mandate to participate in the Great Commission. To see this we need to reassess and redefine our current paradigms, but the changes happening are exciting and awe inspiring. If you find yourself in this category, I am hoping this book will help interpret for you this generation, and affirm that all is not lost: far from it.

Why this book and why now?

For some time now I have been asked to put pen to paper – or more exactly finger to keyboard – and write about global mission. My response has always been to wonder what I can add to what has already been written. As many will tell you, I'm not a missiologist or a theologian. I'm just an ordinary Brit with a passion for global mission, young people and Europe.

However, over the last three years I have been asked more and more to speak and teach on mission mobilisation, and have been asked again and again, 'Have you written what you said in a book?'

'Yes, most of it's in a book,' I reply. 'But it's not written by me! In fact, it was written by Andrew Murray in 1901.'

Recently I have had the growing conviction that what Murray wrote about the challenge of mission is still relevant today and, with a little contemporising, would speak effectively to our postmodern world. As I began reflecting on this, I noticed how I had been mentored and discipled by Andrew Murray over the last twenty years or so.

Shortly after I took on the role of Director of Hull Youth for Christ in the north of England, my wife Denice and I were asked to lead and speak at a youth weekend for St Barnabas Church in Swanland, East Yorkshire. This was our first ever youth weekend and together we were amazed to see how God blessed our ministry among those young people. At the close of the weekend they gave me a copy of Andrew Murray's book *The Ministry of Intercession*. That signed gift from a group of teenagers was my introduction to Andrew Murray, and it has been a continual encouragement to me.

Within weeks of reading it I was on the lookout for other Murray books. While rummaging in a second-hand bookshop I came across a battered copy of his *The Key to the Missionary Problem*.[1] This book is unlike his other titles, of which there were over 240 published, because it was written in response to the great Ecumenical Missionary Conference held in New York in 1900. Even though he was unable to attend, the organisers arranged for transcripts to be sent to Murray, who was in South Africa. His response to the words spoken at the conference, as you will read, was one of passion and a great burden for establishing the Kingdom of God globally.

The driving force of his book is revealed when Murray questions why, when there are millions of Christians in the world, the number of believers involved in global mission is so few. His answer then was the same as it is now: lack of heart. Enthusiasm and passion for the Kingdom is missing because there is so little enthusiasm and passion for the King. Throughout his book Murray commends the efforts being made by careful organisation of limited resources in people and money, but he is at pains to point out that more could be done and achieved if confidence was restored and courage engendered through rediscovery of the presence of a Jesus to whom every heart should beat in loyalty and devotion. The book is filled not only with hope but also warning and continually lays upon believers the responsibility for global mission. It is here that Murray coins the phrase 'The challenge of global mission is a personal one for every believer.'

When I first read Murray's words I could not believe that they were written eighty years previously! Today, they are 102 years old, and they still sound highly charged with passion, warning, hope and prophecy. I pray that they inspire you as much, if not more, as they have discipled me over the last twenty years.

The past rooted in the present

As I have set about contemporising and abridging the words of this great church leader and hero of the faith, I have interlaced them with some material that Greg Reader and I began developing for the European MISSION Congress in 2001.

---

[1] Andrew Murray, *The Key to the Missionary Problem* (Christian Literature Crusade, 1979).

Greg and I met in Austria for a week in July 2001 to write some material that would appear in the congress handbook that December. Within hours of being together we realised how we were only just beginning to disciple young people through the materials we were writing. Over the coming days we began to discover and share that our own journey into mission was one not of career choice, but rather lifestyle. The more we talked and prayed together the more we saw that Jesus developed and discipled his followers towards a Mission Lifestyle.

As a result of this time together we began working on material designed to help young European people discover their place in global mission by personally developing a Mission Lifestyle.

A personal challenge – a Mission Lifestyle

It is my hope that by reading the plea from Andrew Murray and by actioning the practical steps Greg and I are suggesting you will be helped to come to a better understanding of what this Mission Lifestyle is and how far you have come in the process of embracing it.

This book is ordered is such a way as to give you time and space to not only be challenged by the words of Andrew Murray but also to take suggested practical action steps. It is hoped that you will not just read it and move on, but that this book is something to which you will keep coming back, and that upon each return you will see with ease how you have progressed in your pilgrimage into global mission.

Some chapters will need careful private reflection, others will require those around you to listen and pray with you. Still others will spur you on to pray for global mission, make contact and go out in cross-cultural mission, or highlight your need for further training or counsel. All have the prayer attached that you will discover God's will and your place to be a living witness to Jesus.

As you grow in a Mission Lifestyle, I hope that you will be thrilled by the dynamic relationship between the global and local aspects of this lifestyle, and that you will take concrete steps to fulfil your integral role in God's mission. There is vital work to be done, and God intends to do it through us, his people, working together.

Trev Gregory
February 2003

To follow and take part in an online discussion of the issues raised in these pages, please join the forum on www.missionnow.com

Foreword

Mission mobilisation can no longer be a barrage of rapid-fire words, a fast-hitting pep talk attempt to convince people they should sacrifice their life for mission ... 'After all, God had only one son and he was a missionary.' Slogans, and easy simplifications don't cut it any more. Mission mobilisation must be serious, authentic, based on vulnerable relationship, and must realistically paint the world in its full need as well as the Great Commission in its full dimensions. Thus we need this book by Trev Gregory.

For over 25 years I have been seriously involved in the production of mission literature, whether writing articles, essays and editing books to designing covers and selecting printing companies, to move towards the final task of pricing, promoting and distributing these new crown jewels of paper and significance. It is a daunting task and my congratulations to the few publishers who see a future in mission literature for all people and in all situations. Occasionally I have reduced the book business to the following. So what if we get a good manuscript, find a gifted editor, locate the right publisher, design an attractive cover and then promote and sell the book. But what if nobody reads the blessed book? Such concerns dog all good writers and publishers, and they generate restless nights.

By God's goodness, such hopefully will not be the case with this helpful mobilisation book. We are grateful to those who have worked with Trev throughout his entire process of conceiving the idea and writing the concepts, helping to craft chapter titles and content, relevance and application.

Trev rightly states that global mission is changing, but it's not merely our perception of change. Radical changes ripple through the Christian church in mission related to worldview, generations, definitions of 'mission' and 'missionary', the base and object of our sending. Political correctness and the new faces of religious pluralism cut at the very heart of God's mission. Globalisation is here to stay in all it's manifestations – economic, political, cultural, terrorism, world religious, and certainly the Christian faith in global mission. The world has come together at an incredible speed of interconnectedness.

Yes, it is a matter of 'mission … now', but it cannot be just the same old way of being and doing mission. The world has profoundly changed on us, in visible and invisible ways. The multi-headed globalisation hydra requires that we consider the new world disorder. Generational and worldview transformations manifest themselves in ways beyond our control. The sense of being and doing church is changing, and the empowering Spirit of God is putting out a new call for a new missional people of God – whether gathered and scattered.

I well remember two distinct school years in the mid-80's when my son, David, played on his secondary school football (soccer for the Americans!) team. The first year the team was steady and sure, but more in losses than wins. Dramatic changes marked that second year on his team. What was the difference? Simply that his school had just accepted a group of exchange students who came from football playing nations. And they came ready to play with the strong and enthusiastic, though less-skilled, Americans. That second year was exciting to watch, and the infusion of new globalised football blood energized the Americans, and together that multi-ethnic team went on to win the state championship.

To me, this simple micro-story provides a dramatic picture of the new mission world. The significant world mission players come from around the world, for mission is now from all nations to all nations, from everywhere to everywhere. We live and play on a new global team of cross-cultural servants.

We express a full thanks to Trev and team for the courage to speak it out. Now may the book be printed, promoted, sold, bought and read; read to be changed – regardless of our current or future sphere of influence in church and mission. This book was written as part of the life journey and within the context of secular, post-Christian (with it's own particular spiritual search) Europe. We are all on this long march on behalf of the nations – whether in short, medium or long term mission service – purposefully pilgrimaging in the same God-direction, in obedience to the eternal sending and loving Father, Son and Spirit.

William D Taylor, Executive Director
World Evangelical Alliance Missions Commission

About The Contributors

Andrew Murray
Born at Graaff Reinet in South Africa in 1828, Andrew Murray was the son of a church pastor. He was educated for the ministry in Scotland and The Netherlands and was ordained a Dutch Reformed pastor in 1848. Murray not only had a calling for local church leadership, but was also active in global mission, particularly throughout Africa. His fervour for teaching on the believer's devotional life led him to write over 240 books. Murray was the most influential leader of his denomination during the nineteenth century and was an evangelical Christian of international stature. He died in 1917.

Greg Reader
Born in Canada in 1964, Greg grew up in a Christian family, and began following Jesus when he was very young. At nineteen he joined International Teams on a two-year commitment in Austria to deliver Christian literature and relief supplies to Christians in the then communist countries of Central and Eastern Europe. Seventeen years later he was still in Austria with International Teams, having served in a variety of roles, including five years as Europe Regional Co-ordinator. He has also been continually involved in local church work, especially youth

leadership. In 2002 Greg moved with his family to the Philippines, where he is presently serving as a training consultant to International Teams East Asia. He and his wife, Helen, have two children, Eryn and Daniel.

Trev Gregory
Born in Britain in 1961, Trev became a Christian while at school. He was a student of the London Bible College and left there aged twenty-two to become the Director of Hull Youth for Christ for four years. He initiated a prayer project for British Youth for Christ, which was taken on by the Evangelical Alliance and many youth agencies in the UK. He later joined Operation Mobilisation and is currently the International Director for TEMA-MISSION. He is married to Denice and has three children.

Part I

Encountering A Mission Lifestyle

Mission As Lifestyle

Shortly after the fall of the Berlin Wall I prayer-walked from London to Berlin with a group of young people from Britain, Germany, France and The Netherlands. Each day we would walk for around seven hours, stay in local Christian homes, and lead prayer concerts in the evening. Each Sunday we rested.

The last Sunday rest was in a small village just over the former border in East Germany. During the afternoon a German prayer-walker called Thomas and I went for a walk around the former communist village and were struck at how time had appeared to stand still. People still fetched water from a communal pump, as few had in-house plumbing. Grass was still being cut with the scythe – something neither of us had ever seen before! Thomas was struck with awe and almost disbelief at the way in which so many East German people had lived for so long while he and other West Germans had 'advanced'. The two lifestyles were almost opposites.

Gathered around the village pond was a group of teenagers. One of them was showing off to his friends his latest set of clothes. He was dressed in black Wrangler jeans and a T-shirt displaying the logo of the heavy metal band AC/DC. Thomas and I went over to speak with them. With Thomas as my interpreter, the boy with the new clothes asked if I liked them? I responded that he looked good in them, 'very Western'.

He immediately took out a copy of a heavy metal music magazine and turned to a photo of AC/DC wearing similar jeans and T-shirts. 'Yes! Western,' he proclaimed excitedly. 'I am now Western. See, I dress Western, listen to AC/DC. I live a Western life.' As he finished and Thomas translated for me, the boy's friends shouted their agreement and approval.

Standing in a village that was living forty years behind the rest of Western Europe with a group of local teenagers insisting that, because they could now buy Western clothes and listen to Western music, they were indeed Western, Thomas and I entered into a long conversation during which we could share our life stories and elements of our Christian lifestyles.

Which lifestyle?

Today we readily use the term 'lifestyle' to describe a way of life or style of living that reflects the attitudes, values and actions of a person or group. When the word became popular a generation ago, a number of critics objected to it as voguish and superficial, perhaps because it appeared to elevate habits of consumption, dress and recreation to categories in a system of social classification. None the less, the word has proved durable and useful, perhaps because it is now seen as describing not only consumer choice or expectation, but because it also explains social values and behaviour.

Look along a news-stand – there are magazines for different lifestyles. Or enter the virtual reality realm of the Internet and you soon discover and can become part of online communities that view life from the perspective of different lifestyle choices. Contained in the pages of these magazines or online communities are not only ads for consumer products which are essential for the chosen lifestyle, but also a set of localised rules, mores and morals.

Furthermore, in the world today there are many lifestyles to choose from. Each is not separate or in isolation from the others, but each has its differences and focuses. One common agreement between lifestyles is that the world is not what it should be, but agreeing on what can and should be done about this is another matter. We can't even agree on what is wrong, let alone how it can be made right!

- Is democracy the answer?
- Economic prosperity?
- Is hope to be found in the defence of human rights?
- The fight for the environment?
- The fight for my own nation?
- Is it to be found in old religions, new religious movements, or in the rejection of all belief in God?
- Is there even any hope at all?

Within so many competing voices and visions, one voice rings true. This voice tells us what is wrong, why it's wrong and how it will be made right. When people listen to this voice and follow it they find themselves changed, reconciled to God and to each other, and filled to overflowing with new life and purpose.

This voice is for everyone. That's why Jesus told his disciples to train and teach everyone they met, both near and far. His way of life isn't 'just any old' way of life – it is life itself. His commands are not just another set of rules – they are words that bring healing, reconciliation, justice and hope. Without these words there is no hope. Without this way of life there is only a road to failure and death. That is why it is so crucial that everyone everywhere should hear these words and see this way of life. That is why Jesus sent his disciples out as he did: he called them to a Mission Lifestyle. And it's why he sends us. Jesus' call to mission is as clear today as it was then: he calls us to a Mission Lifestyle.

The mission is global: Jesus wants everyone, both near and far, to see and hear. The mission is also local, for just as the Father sent Jesus to a specific place at a specific time, so we are sent into specific contexts to witness.

If you are a follower of Christ you have already been sent into mission. God has placed you in your family, in a particular neighbourhood, in a specific school or job. He has put you among people who are similar to you, with whom it is relatively easy to communicate clearly. But in close proximity to you are also many people of other cultures, colours and creeds, and God expects you and other Christians to be a clear witness to them as well. And don't forget the rest of the world!

Today the world is more interconnected than ever before, which should be a reminder to us that God's vision and call is global and applies to all peoples everywhere, all the way to the ends of the earth. If we are to live consistently as God's people we must recognise these realities and allow them to change every aspect of our lives – our giving, our learning, our work, our attitudes, our loyalties, our words, and even our locations. This is what it means to embrace a Mission Lifestyle. It's not easy – Jesus never said it would be. But he did say that he would be with his disciples day in and day out, reminding us of the mission he has given us and the commitments we have made, and encouraging us on throughout a lifetime of learning and service.

Encountering a Mission Lifestyle

As we have already seen, a lifestyle is shaped by a person's identity, beliefs and actions. So too is a Mission Lifestyle. Let's therefore take a closer look at what a Mission Lifestyle encompasses.

Firstly, a Mission Lifestyle shapes identity in so far as it tells the individual who he or she is and where he or she fits into God's Kingdom and eternal plan. Throughout his letters Paul's aim is to instruct his readers, but also remind them of who they are in the sight of God. He wants them to know who they are in order that they live, act and relate to each other accordingly.

The opening chapter of Paul's letter to the Colossians is a good example. What is most stunning about this letter is that the believers in Colossae had never met Paul or heard him preach: he had never visited them. Their local church had been planted by one of Paul's converts, Epaphras. Therefore, for me, what Paul actually writes is all the more intriguing and interesting. Before sharing secrets of his prayer life with the Colossians, he identifies this community of believers as 'holy and faithful brothers in Christ' (Col. 1:2). This is their identity.

He then goes further and says:

> We always thank God, the Father of our Lord Jesus Christ, when we pray for you, because we have heard of your faith in Christ Jesus and of the love you have for all the saints (Col. 1:3–4).

Paul goes on to build upon the Colossians' identity and puts this into the context of how the gospel is bearing fruit in their community and across the world (Col. 1:5–6). He also talks about the historical context in which the Colossians received and heard the gospel from Epaphras (Col. 1:7–8).

He then reveals what he has been praying for the Colossians and mixes the ideas of their identity and history alongside images of their future, hopes and the reality of how God sees them.

> For this reason, since the day we heard about you, we have not stopped praying for you and asking God to fill you with the knowledge of his will through all spiritual wisdom and understanding. And we pray this in order that you may live a life worthy of the Lord and may please him in every way: bearing fruit in every good work, growing in the knowledge of God, being strengthened with all power according to his glorious might so that you may have great endurance and patience, and joyfully giving thanks to the Father who has qualified you to share in the inheritance of the saints in the kingdom of light. For he has rescued us from the dominion of darkness and brought us into the kingdom of the Son he loves, in whom we have redemption, the forgiveness of sins (Col. 1:9–14).

From here Paul writes of the supremacy of Christ over all creation and of how our identity is embedded in Christ's, who is the head of the church (Col. 1:15–20). He then once again places this in a wider historical and global context and illustrates the background to this community of believers' identity as being part of an eternal plan (Col. 1:21–23).

Finally, Paul ends the chapter by sharing personally from his own life, experience and ministry (Col. 1:24–29). This is not to boast about his own achievements, but rather is an expression of his wanting to show how his understanding of his own identity has shaped his life and actions. For Paul, his lifestyle encompasses his identity, beliefs and actions: his whole life.

> We proclaim him, admonishing and teaching everyone with all wisdom, so that we may present everyone perfect in

Christ. To this end I labour, struggling with all this energy, which so powerfully works in me (Col. 1:28–29).

This now brings us to the second aspect of a Mission Lifestyle: belief.

Until recently the West treated faith and, subsequently, a person's lifestyle as separate and distinct from other aspects of life. The death of faith in the public arena was just one of the consequences of modernity. I once heard that the Chief Executive of McDonald's had stated to a group of young executives 'On Sunday I believe in God, my family and McDonald's. From Monday to Saturday the order is reversed.'

But such compartmentalisation is getting more and more difficult to sustain, as we are now in transition from modernity to postmodernity, and it is evermore noticeable that the faith aspect of life has once again affected every part of our lives, work, actions and identities. As I meet with many young people across Europe, one trend is sure: they are wrestling with their faith because they are searching for its relevance to today's world.

Perhaps this might begin to provide an answer as to why people are more open to Christianity and spiritual matters, but at the same time there is an increased intolerance and abandonment if the faith is perceived as not working. By thinking in terms of lifestyle we more readily see how integrated faith and belief should be into all of life.

Faith has to work or the whole lifestyle is called into question. Some time ago I was asked to teach at a mission training school on prayer teams. When I arrived, the leader took me to one side and asked what my position was on territorial spirits. Knowing that the mission training school was charismatic and wondering if he was concerned about my views, I asked why he had asked me the question. The leader said, 'We have been deeply entrenched in the territorial spirit teaching from the USA and have organised much of our mission around it. However, ten years on, I am of the conclusion that it does not work. So am wanting to know what does.' This reply illustrates how a lifestyle set upon a belief has to work in action.

The third facet of Mission Lifestyle, action, is interdependent on the other two, as indeed are the two facets discussed above, identity and belief. Actions undertaken of a Mission Lifestyle flow out from the exploration and understanding of one's identity and belief. Similarly, identity and belief must be placed into action in order to remain relevant and alive. It was the Apostle James who wrote 'Faith by itself, if it is not accompanied by action, is dead' (Jas. 2:17).

Once these three elements are functioning together a clearer understanding of a Mission Lifestyle is allowed. A Mission Lifestyle makes it possible to move away from the either/ors which have stifled thought, unity and action in Europe in the advancement of the gospel for so long. Mission Lifestyle allows theology and missiology, evangelism and social action, secular and sacred, and local and global to sit alongside each other.

Therefore a Mission Lifestyle includes an active interplay between thought and opinions, perception and worldview. In other words, a Mission Lifestyle gives meaning to the way the world is perceived, which then gives meaning, reason and a reference place to identity, belief and action.

At the same time there is a closing of the chasm between secular and sacred, as both are seen of equal value and relevance. Under modernity the calling to a missionary vocation was seen and often spoken of as higher than secular employment. Development of a Mission Lifestyle in no way diminishes the fact that some are called to missionary vocations or suggests that all are missionaries; rather it expresses the belief that every believer is involved in global mission irrespective of vocation or employment.

Recent European Union studies on employment suggest that in the twenty-first century the average person will have on average four career changes during his or her years of employment. This is three more than my father's generation, and this is a trend which many mission agencies are only just beginning to comprehend. When this is translated into global mission terms, the increase in short-term mission is placed into context.

This trend might also go some way to explaining why some people are 'mission dipping'. I first heard the term 'mission dipping' from a German couple, who were explaining to me their Mission Lifestyle. They were both trained teachers and sensed God's calling into teaching and cross-cultural mission in a 10/40 Window country. Their Mission Lifestyle pattern was to spend up to five years in this Central Asian country and then a similar period in Germany teaching.

Through adopting and developing a Mission Lifestyle, the competitiveness between local and global is laid to rest, as both are encompassed in one. At present, I see that many individuals have made this transition, but the outworking within mission agencies and church structures is slower because such a paradigm shift has implications on strategy and structure. It is no longer the case that a choice has to be made between global mission and local ministry. Both are not mutually exclusive, and both are of equal validity. Living a Mission Lifestyle means that by being a living witness locally one can minister globally in global mission. The two are one. The phrase John Wesley coined in the 1700s to express his sense of the global and local nature of the gospel and his part in proclaiming it – 'The world is my parish' – sounds even more like a prophecy being fulfilled, as believers today believe it and live within it.

As local and global come together along with the secular and sacred, so too do evangelism and social responsibility. The July 1974 Lausanne Covenant (the result of a series of meetings and studies initiated by Billy Graham) is of strategic importance to evangelical believers across the globe. One of the components of the Lausanne Covenant was the evangelical recognition of the importance of social action. Up until this time many evangelicals had been of the opinion that social action should not to be a significant feature of church life, and this opinion was put into practice.

The Lausanne Covenant firstly defines the verb 'to evangelise' as:

> to spread the good news that Jesus Christ died for our sins and was raised from the dead according to the Scriptures, and that as the reigning Lord he now offers the forgiveness of sins and the liberating gifts of the Spirit to all who repent and believe.

It then affirms social responsibility in the following way:

> We ... should share [God's] concern for justice and reconciliation throughout human society and for the liberation of men and women from every kind of oppression. Because men and women are made in the image of God, every person, regardless of race, religion, colour, culture, class, sex or age, has an intrinsic dignity because of which he or she should be respected and served, not exploited ... When people receive Christ they are born again into his kingdom and must seek not only to exhibit but also to spread its righteousness in the midst of an unrighteous world. The salvation we claim should be transforming us in the totality of our personal and social responsibilities. Faith without works is dead.

From trips to the recycling bins with glass, paper and old clothes to supporting Greenpeace or Amnesty International, as well as being more globally aware and informed, for many it is increasingly becoming second nature to be privately socially responsible.

More and more local churches are also developing both evangelism and social responsibility programmes. In city after city across Europe local churches are developing integrated activities where evangelism and social action are equal partners. In the past the church has done evangelism and the church has done social ministry – but not always together, like now. Such promotion of social and spiritual wellbeing as equally important and interdependent aspects of mission is based on the belief that meeting social needs opens doors to sharing faith and spiritual nurture enhances the outcomes of social interventions. From running a soup kitchen meal that begins with a devotional or a parenting support group that uses Christian teaching, to other programmes that take a less direct, more informal approach, the goal is to cultivate personal relationships and look for opportunities to initiate a spiritual dialogue to invite people to church services or special events where they can hear the gospel message. As this merging happens, so the chasm between evangelism and social responsibility is filled.

As we have seen, developing a Mission Lifestyle happens on many fronts in a person's life, through permeating the conscious and unconscious to shape and determine identity, belief and action. One essential and key need in its development is a biblical understanding of mission. It is this that we turn to now.

2

Mission – What Is It?

The most significant foundation for a Mission Lifestyle is a clear understanding, acceptance and belief in God's plan for the whole of creation as portrayed throughout Scripture. As we have seen in the previous chapter, such a belief will shape identity and action.

Many have written biblical assessments of mission and their thoughts fill many thousands of books. I am limiting myself here to one chapter, a swift jog to set out an understanding of mission and how it connects to a Mission Lifestyle.

I remember a late-night conversation I had with a fellow student while at London Bible College. We were debating what Britain has to do with Bosnia; or Hull with Hydrabad. Our heated debate centred on the responsibility of churches and individuals to be involved in communities far beyond their own. At the time I was eager to understand if I had a place in global mission, as I felt my calling was to youth work in the UK, and was searching for an answer. I began to realise during this uncomfortable discussion that I had narrowly defined my calling and that my tunnel vision was hindering me from seeing God's wider global universal plan for humanity and the whole earth. My self-centred worldview and faith was severely challenged as I wrestled with the age-old questions first voiced by the early church father Tertullian centuries before.

Why should we concern ourselves with human tragedies in places like Sarajevo or Ethiopia? Why should holocausts like those that took place in Rwanda or Indonesia touch our lives when it is obvious that the Sovereign Lord has placed us in a secure society away from these dangers and other winds of adversity? Should we worry about restoring democracy to Haiti, Sierra Leone or Iraq? Should we be asking questions about human rights in China, Yemen or Egypt? Should we be concerned with the plight of emigrants? Why should we load ourselves with the burdens of the world and allow ourselves to be disturbed by statistics of war, disease and poverty? Why should the turmoil of the world disrupt the tranquillity of our hearts and surroundings? Why should we go, share, preach and disciple people of other cultures and religions of the world? Why should we seek to rise up and mobilise our best people to serve the poor, the needy, the unloved, the homeless and the lost?

I grappled with my friend and as his voice rose, he offered reason after reason, argument after argument, for taking up our responsibility. At each one I grew more and more unsatisfied with the logic. Then quietly, almost muttering, he said, 'I guess there is only one compelling reason: "For God so loved the world."' With these words we both stopped and wondered as such a simple, obvious and profound truth sank into not just our minds but our lives also. That night's discussion changed my understanding of global mission and so began my quest to discover a balanced view and belief based upon Scripture.

Let's begin our jog with a study of what mission means.

Mission – the word

The word 'mission' is derived from the Latin verb *mittere*, which means 'to send'. There is a picture attached to the meaning – that of a person or group that has been assigned to and sent to perform a task.

The New Testament uses two Greek words in specific ways in relationship to the ministry of the gospel in both word and deed. The first Greek word, *diakonia*, is translated 'mission' in Acts 12:25. Meanwhile, the second Greek word, *apostolos* (the noun form of the verb *apostellein*, which means to send out or send away), which we translate as 'apostle', is used to denote someone sent on the service of another, or someone sent with a commission.

Missio Dei (literally 'the mission of God') is a Latin phrase used by one of the early church fathers, Saint Augustine, to clarify who was doing the sending. He used this term to illustrate how God the Son was sent by God the Father. Throughout the early church period *Missio Dei* was understood as denoting everything God does for the communication of the message of salvation and everything the church is sent to achieve this in the world.

Implied within the 'sending' of *Missio Dei* is incarnation. Through the incarnation of Jesus we can begin to see the synergy between the Godhead, history and eternity, local and global. The incarnation is perhaps the most focused expression of the dynamic relationship between the local and global aspects of mission. Jesus was a Jew who lived and worked among the Jewish people in Galilee and Judea early in the first century. In other words, the Father sent the Son to a particular place, at a particular time, to live and work among a specific people. You can't get much more local than that! And yet the life, death and resurrection of Jesus are of eternal, global and even cosmic significance, for it is on that basis (and on that basis alone) that God offers salvation to all people of all ages, no matter where they are in the world, what culture they are a part of or what language they speak. It is also on that basis that we are able to look forward to the day when God will bring evil to an end and make all things new.

This is a global message, worked out practically in a myriad of local contexts, as Christians go to all peoples in this world and bear witness to the historical life, death and resurrection of Jesus, to the new life he has given us personally, and to the hope we have for eternity. In just the same way as Jesus was sent by the Father to live within a local context, so are we. Yet his actions and life have had not only a global impact but a historic and eternal one also.

During the twentieth century some liberal scholars used *Missio Dei* in a way which excluded evangelism and focused solely on justice issues. In reaction to this, some Christians became wary of using the term at all, unless its meaning was narrowed to the task of world evangelisation and the planting and nurturing of churches among non-Christians. More recently, primarily since the Lausanne Covenant, a more holistic understanding of 'the mission of God' has begun to emerge.

We can now stop for a moment and reflect on the following statements:

- *Missio Dei* – God's mission – began with the Trinity, was embodied in Jesus, is the responsibility of believers throughout the ages, and will find fulfilment in the ultimate establishment of God's Kingdom.
- Debates among Christians have led to many believing that proclamational evangelism and social action are mutually exclusive definitions of mission. In reality, word and deed are integrally related in the communication of the gospel and the practice of mission.

- The numerical growth of the church is only part of the *Missio Dei*. God certainly desires as many people as possible to come to a saving knowledge of him and join the community of his people. But God wants to accomplish much more than just bringing together a collection of converts.
- God didn't send his Son into the whole world, but to a particular place at a specific point in time and to work among a particular people. While this act has global implications and impact, it is only when felt and worked out at the local level that it holds real meaning for people.

Mission, then, is summoning the disobedient to turn to God. It is done from the context of a life where God is truly worshipped, the faithful built up and compassion demonstrated.

Mission in the Bible

When thinking about a biblical basis for mission we need to read Jesus' words in Matthew 28 ...

> God authorized and commanded me to commission you: Go out and train everyone you meet, far and near, in this way of life, marking them by baptism in the threefold name: Father, Son, and Holy Spirit (MSG).

Mark 16 ...

> Go into the world. Go everywhere and announce the Message of God's good news to one and all. Whoever believes and is baptized is saved; whoever refuses to believe is damned (MSG).

and his most famous words in John 3 ...

This is how much God loved the world: He gave his Son, his one and only Son. And this is why: so that no one need be destroyed; by believing in him anyone can have a whole and lasting life (MSG).

within the context of what has been revealed earlier in the Bible, because Jesus built upon and developed this. We need to go right back to the beginning, because the story of the Bible is the story of mission.

Chris Wright, former Principal of All Nations Christian College, sums up the biblical story in just four major events: creation, the Fall, redemption and new creation.[1]

Creation – Genesis 1

'In the beginning God created the heavens and the earth.' Creation is the beginning of history and therefore the beginning of mission. Genesis tells us that God's original purpose was for the world and humanity. The world is described as good, it has order and value, and evil was not originally in it.

Meanwhile, humanity was the crown of God's creation, created in God's own image, in a way that the animals and the rest of creation were not. While dependant on God, humans were created as morally responsible beings, accountable to him. The creation story also shows that all humanity is equal; all have dignity; and are made to work, rest and be productive and creative. We are stewards of creation, which means we are responsible for the world's resources.

The Fall – Genesis 3

The Fall, like creation, was a definite event in history. It was caused by sin. Sin spoils every relationship possible

[1] Chris Wright, *The Use of the Bible in Social Ethics* (Grove, 1984).

for humans – their relationship with God, with each other, with themselves, with creation. Sin is universal – it has affected all the people of the world since the Fall; it corrupts every personality; it has affected the whole of human history; and, because humans are communal beings, it has contaminated corporate structures.

Redemption

Sin came crashing in at the Fall, but this has not stopped God's purposes, as we can see from the rest of the Bible. If anything it strengthened his resolve in mission.

To 'redeem' something is to buy it back. Jesus said that he came to `give his life as a ransom for many' (Mark 10:45). The picture is that of a slave being freed by payment of a ransom. Humanity is said to be `in slavery to sin'. Even if we want to give up sinning, we cannot do so. But by his life, death and resurrection Jesus paid the price, the ransom, that would set us free.

Christians are therefore `the redeemed', just as the Israelites who had been brought out of slavery in Egypt were `the redeemed' in the Old Testament. Paul urges his readers to consider the price that was paid for their redemption and give themselves wholeheartedly in service to God. He also urges his readers not to fall back into the old ways but to allow God to rid them of the marks left by their former slavery to sin. We've been set free, but this world is still in bondage, so the full experience of our freedom must wait until Jesus returns and leads us into the perfect freedom of living in the presence of God.

Chris Wright further suggests that redemption in history can be divided into three stages:

1   God and Israel – God's mission through Israel – from the promise given to Abraham to the coming of Jesus.

2 The coming of Jesus – God's mission through Jesus – from his birth to his resurrection and ascension.

3 The church – God's mission through the church – from Christ's ascension until the Second Coming.

New Creation

Like the other three biblical events, this fourth event builds on the others. The creation of a new heaven and earth marks the end of mission activity because God's purpose is fulfilled. Not only are humanity and creation transformed, but also humanity is aware of the gravity and consequences of sin.

Understanding the detail of the backdrop

We can now use this brief biblical overview as a background in studying Scripture passages alongside the following questions. Who is God fulfilling his mission through? How do they act or speak? And finally, who will benefit if the mission is fulfilled, and in what ways? In Genesis 12:1–3 God calls Abram as a servant pioneer to go where he leads, and as a result Abram will be blessed, as will 'all peoples on earth'. Some 500 years later God speaks to Moses on Mount Sinai and instructs him to address the whole nation, as God is about to reiterate and develop further the calling to Abram.

In Exodus 19:3–6 Moses is told to remind the Israelites of the way God had graciously redeemed them from slavery in Egypt. God had not only brought them out of Egypt but had also protected them like an eagle protects its young on its wings. This first generation of redeemed Israelites knew from first-hand personal knowledge what God had done for them. He had visibly demonstrated that

they were a favoured nation. It is this that forms the very
centre and essence of the calling now being given. 'Now if
you obey me fully and keep my covenant,' the Lord tells
Moses to tell the people, 'then out of all nations you will be
my treasured possession' (Exod. 19:5).

Throughout this passage and continually in the Old
Testament there is no suggestion of a lack of love for other
nations or peoples; rather there is an emphasis on the special relationship of God with the people of Israel. There is a
hint that because the people of Israel were called to live
according to God's laws and commands as a 'kingdom of
priests' and as a 'holy nation' that they were doing this on
behalf of all humanity, not just for themselves. It was as a
kingdom of priests that Israel's role in global mission
became explicit. The whole nation was to function in a
mediatory role between the nations of the world and God.
In fact, there are direct echoes of this calling in 1 Peter 2:9,
where the New Testament church is charged with taking
the mantle from Israel as a priesthood of all believers.

As a 'holy nation' Israel was to be wholly for the Lord.
Absolutely his. The Israelites were to be set apart not only
in their lives but also in their service. Their calling by God
was for service towards God as their King, but also for service to the nations of the world. They were to be a nation
set apart for all the times and for the entire world. Instead,
almost immediately the people of Israel not only ask
Moses to mediate for them as their priest, but begin to act
for as a pious club rather than sharing God's blessing,
truth and gifts.

When Peter came to use such similar expressions in his
letter to Gentile believers, he did so quite deliberately, as
the church had now succeeded Israel in this mediatory
role. His use, then, of Exodus 19 is obvious and clear. The
reason why God calls his people, the church, in 1 Peter 2:9
to be a chosen race, a royal priesthood, a holy nation, a

people belonging to God, is so that they might announce, declare and serve the peoples of the world as God's missionaries and witnesses. His hopes as set out in Exodus 19 for Israel now rest on the church. These expressions are more than mere badges or titles; rather they are for the purpose of declaring God's deeds and calling people into his light.

Let us take one more passage and apply our questions in order to see how the four biblical events not only link and hinge together but also explain for us God's global mission purposes. My lecturer from my time at London Bible College, Peter Hicks, suggested in a series of lectures on the book of Revelation that it contains not a constant chronological line of events, but is rather a set of images and metaphors, which each point to and build on a central image of heaven. Therefore, in Revelation 5:9–10 there is the first mention in the heavenly hymn of 'every tribe and language and people and nation'. Later, in 7:9–10, after the opening of the sixth seal, there is a return to the heavenly scene, but now 'every nation, tribe, people and language' is physically present.

Both through the hymn in chapter 5 and their presence in chapter 7 it becomes clear that it is because of the sacrificial death of Christ that it is possible for 'every nation, tribe, people and language' to be presented to God. His work on the cross was sufficient for all humanity and neither heaven nor the new creation will be complete without the whole make-up of humanity being present. Another perspective on this is that although Christ's work is sufficient, it is not complete until 'every nation, tribe, people and language' is gathered around the throne in 'a multitude'. Therefore as part of the church we are called and commissioned to serve and live to this end.

Theologians and missiologists like David Bosch, Lesslie Newbigin, N.T. Wright, John Stott and many others agree that, ultimately, the concept of mission is about God's efforts to redeem this fallen and dying world, eradicate evil and establish his just and loving reign for all eternity. Of course, this is mission in the broadest sense of the term, but if we are properly to understand and fulfil our role in mission we must not lose sight of this context. God has set the aims, he has worked out the strategy, he is the Prime Mover, he is the Resourcer, and he will accomplish his purposes. Let us now begin to determine our role and place in them.

3

The Face of Global Mission

Last words are important.

Each time I lifted Nelson Mandela's autobiography I had the question in my mind: how did he ever forgive his persecutors and move on? Throughout the book he pieces together an answer, but it is on the last page that he really shares what is in his heart, which not only shows his own motivation, but lays for his readers a personal vision and goal for the future.

> It was during those long and lonely years that my hunger for the freedom of my own people became the hunger for the freedom of all people, black and white. I knew as well as I knew anything that the oppressor must be liberated just as surely as the oppressed. A man who takes away another man's freedom is a prisoner of hatred, he is locked behind the bars of prejudice and narrow-mindedness. I am not truly free if I am taking away someone else's freedom, just as surely as I am not free when my freedom is taken away from me. The oppressed and the oppressor alike are robbed of their humanity.[1]

---

[1] Nelson Mandela, *Long Walk to Freedom* (Little, Brown, 1994), p. 617.

Similarly, in the sporting world, a coach spends weeks, months or even years training a team, but it is often those last few words before the players step on to the pitch which make the difference by focusing their energies, lifting their spirits and spurring them on.

Likewise, when we are separated from a loved one, it is often the last thing that he or she says to us to which we cling in our memories – a final snapshot of that person and his or her hopes for us. When Jesus left the Apostles to return to his Father the last thing he said to them was:

> you will receive power when the Holy Spirit comes on you; and you will be my witnesses in Jerusalem, and in all Judea and Samaria, and to the ends of the earth (Acts 1:8).

Last words are very, very important.

Jesus said these words to his Apostles, who had a very unique role in the founding of the church, so we need to be careful in how we apply the words to ourselves. Perhaps, rather than putting ourselves in the place of the Apostles, we would do better to compare ourselves with those people in Jerusalem, Judea, Samaria and beyond who later came to believe in Jesus through the Apostles' witness. And yet it is fair to say that the call of these people was essentially an extension of the mission with which Jesus charged the Apostles, since it is clear from the New Testament that God intended his people to go on bearing witness to Jesus in their own home communities, while also extending that witness to the very ends of the earth. Our call today is no different, because he wants all people, everywhere, to come to know him.

Same calling, different world

Although our calling is the same, the world of the twenty-first century is vastly different from that of the first century. Social commentators agree with business and leadership consultant Peter F. Drucker that no other 'century in recorded history has experienced so many social transformations and such radical ones as the twentieth century. They, I submit, may turn out to be the most significant events of this, our century, and its lasting legacy.' He concludes his article with the recommendation and prediction that 'If the twentieth century was one of social transformations, the twenty-first century needs to be one of social and political innovations, whose nature cannot be so clear to us now as their necessity.'[2]

One transformation that Western Europe particularly has to come to terms with is the increased mobility of people globally since the 1950s. As a result of a colonial past, throughout Europe today we have ever-increasing multi-cultural communities taking root. Moreover, today we are witnessing increased numbers seeking economic security and sanctuary in Europe. As Europe faces up to its multi-cultural nature, diversity amongst its own peoples and acceptance of people from outside its borders, another factor is introduced, which the Christian community has to address – the impact that this is having on our mission strategy and structure. From Arnhem in The Netherlands to Leicester in England to Zurich in Switzerland, I can cross over cultural borders without crossing a geographical one. As one German missiologist commented at a conference I attended, 'The world has come to Europe.'

But there are more, profoundly broader, social transformations taking place. Not only has technology and scientific achievement led to a changed world – religion has played an important role too. The face of Christian mission has also changed because of its accomplishments

---

[2] Peter F. Drucker, 'Age of Social Transformation', *The Atlantic Monthly* (November 1994). Go to the back issues database at www.atlanticmonthly.com

across the globe. The preface to Chris Wright's book *The Uniqueness of Jesus* opens with the words: 'The most striking reality in the history of the church in the twentieth century was undoubtedly the growth of Christianity outside the Western world.'[3] The fact is that there are three-to-one more Christians in Africa, Asia and Latin America than in Europe and North America or Australia.

This incredible growth means, suggests Philip Jenkins in his recently published book *The Next Christendom*, that 'we are currently living through one of the transforming moments in the history of religion worldwide'.[4] For the last five centuries the story of Christianity has been inextricably bound up with that of Europe and European-derived civilisations overseas. Yet over the last century this focus has shifted from the northern to the southern hemisphere. Therefore, says Jenkins, 'to visualise a typical contemporary Christian, we should think of a woman living in a village in Nigeria'.[5] Meanwhile, the Kenyan scholar John Mbiti has observed, 'the centres of the church's universality are no longer in Geneva, Rome, Athens, Paris London or New York, but Kinshasa, Buenos Aires, Addis Ababa and Manila'.[6]

Mission types

In embracing a Mission Lifestyle, then, it is important for us to consider and take into account these changes as

---

[3] Chris Wright, *The Uniqueness of Jesus* (Monarch, 2001), p. 7.

[4] Philip Jenkins, *The Next Christendom: The Coming of Global Christianity* (Oxford University Press, 2002), p. 2.

[5] Ibid.

[6] John Mbiti quoted in ibid. Original quotation from Kwame Bediako, *Christianity in Africa* (Edinburgh University Press, 1995), p. 154.

they impact our view of and approach to global mission. However great and significant global transformations are, each of the following 'types' of mission described below has a biblical precedent, and each has its own unique challenges. Therefore we must remember that our calling is the same as that of the first-century believers. The world is different, but the needs and approaches are often similar.

Mission in my own country, among people of my own culture

The early Christians could be found in the Temple, the synagogues and the market-places of Judea. They were integrated into Jewish society, and yet they were obviously different, often painfully so. How is it for us today in our own immediate surroundings, among people with whom we can relate and communicate with relative ease due to shared language and cultural background? In this context, the difference the gospel makes should contrast with everyday normalities. When we are clearly different from those who expect us to be similar to them, all kinds of questions will be raised as to why. Peter tells us to 'Be ready to speak up and tell anyone who asks why you're living the way you are' (1 Peter 3:15, MSG).

There's a further challenge here: a challenge of identity. When we become Christians we gain a new identity and a new home. We are now God's people, making us different from those who share our particular human culture. It is this difference that needs to become evident in the context we once saw as home, and if we are to be effective witnesses we need to be able to explain the reason for it.

Mission in my own country, among people of other cultures

On the day of Pentecost there were people from all over the Roman Empire and beyond present in Jerusalem. And because of the working of the Holy Spirit they all heard the gospel in their own language! Many of those people were Jews who were living in other parts of the world and who spoke the local languages. Others were converts to Judaism from other ethnic groups. The main point is that early on we find Christians reaching out across cultural and linguistic barriers. This was, for them, a very radical step, and not without controversy.

Today, we are faced with the reality that God has brought millions of people from hundreds of nations and cultures together in the major urban centres of the world. It is possible for the majority of Christians to come into contact with a great number of the peoples of the world without ever going anywhere else! This is a tremendous opportunity and a daunting challenge. When we are somehow different from others in our own culture, people will often want to know why. But when people from other cultures see me as different from themselves, it is natural to assume that this is simply because our cultures are different. The big problem is that many times they are right! The challenge is to find out how to connect cross-culturally in ways that allow the unique transforming power of the gospel to shine through, once again provoking those questions of why we Christians are the way we are.

Mission in another country, among people of my own culture

Whenever the Apostle Paul came to a new city, the first place he went was to the synagogue. It seems that there were Jews in almost every city of the Roman Empire at that time! And Paul, even though he was specifically called to preach the gospel to non-Jews, still spent much time and energy trying to convince his fellow Jews everywhere that Jesus was the Messiah.

It is normal today for major cities to have eighty or more recognisable, established communities of distinct ethnic groups. Almost regardless of where you come from, if you spend some time exploring a city you will meet people living there who share your language and culture. And just as with any other people living in the world, God wants them to believe in and follow him. Sometimes it is through the witness of local Christians that churches spring up in these communities, sometimes it is because people were Christians before they came, and other times it is because Christians from 'back home' were sent as missionaries to their own people in another part of the world.

An important thing for people in this type of ministry to keep in mind is that, even though they are specifically focused on 'their own' people, as Christians they are still responsible for their witness to people around them of other cultures. It is refreshing to hear of Filipino churches, for example, in various countries around the world that are beginning to take seriously their responsibility to share their hope with people from other ethnic groups living in the vicinity. The same is true of many other nationalities.

It is also important to remember that even though 'expatriates' usually keep many of their cultural distinctives, living outside of their homeland none the less influences them. Often the changes are subtle and difficult at first to perceive. But especially then it is a mistake to think that someone from 'back home' will not have difficulties integrating into a community just because its members share a common language and broad cultural similarities. The experience of the expatriate community is different from the community 'back home' and therefore its values and sensitivities have also become somewhat different. It is these subtle differences, precisely because they are often unexpected, which can be the most difficult to adjust to.

Mission in another country, among people of other cultures

This is what, for most people, immediately comes to mind when they hear the word 'mission'. For the missionary this situation is full of challenges – adjustments to new surroundings, cultural adaptation and language learning, to name just a few. A more subtle challenge is similar to what was mentioned earlier concerning cross-cultural ministry: when people sense a difference in us, they are most likely going to assume that it is primarily due to cultural distinctions, rather than the result of the transforming work of God in our lives.

Paul's words have often been a source of motivation for those facing such challenges:

> It has always been my ambition to preach the gospel where Christ was not known, so that I would not be building on someone else's foundation. Rather, as it is written: 'Those who were not told about him will see, and those who have not heard will understand' (Rom. 15:20–21).

Since there are still places in the world where there has been little or no Christian witness, and still people who have had little or no contact with the gospel, this type of ministry continues to be of utmost importance in mission. We need many, many more harvest hands, from nations all over the world, to follow the example of Paul and reach out with the hope of the gospel to those who have not yet heard in any way.

But there is an exciting dynamic to international mission that has been emerging more and more over the last century. Many parts of the world that had, only one or two hundred years ago, little or no gospel witness, are now resonating with vibrant, growing communities of Christians. And these communities are joining in the task of reaching out to all people everywhere! Now when we get involved in ministry in another part of the world, we, more often than not, have to take into account who else is working there, what churches already exist, and how we can best work together. Partnership has become the word of the day, and rightly so, because it reflects the fact that God's family are made up of a plurality of peoples, and that through the gospel we are enabled to experience profound unity in the face of rich diversity. We can learn from each other and mutually support each other as we each contribute our strengths and are helped in our weaknesses, thus enhancing the effectiveness of our witness.

Global mission is becoming increasingly 'from everywhere to everywhere'. While in the eighteenth and nineteenth centuries mission was seen primarily as Western Christians going to non-Western parts of the world, the twentieth century witnessed an amazing shift. Indigenous Christians in lands that Western Christians had for more than 200 years referred to as 'the mission field' began taking more and more initiative in reaching out not only to their own communities but also to people of other cultures as well. Non-Western churches began sending missionaries to other parts of the world – even to the West! In fact, during the twentieth century it became increasingly recognised that the West is itself a mission field. Today it is no longer valid to divide the world into 'the mission field' and 'the home base'. The mission field is everywhere, and the home base is everywhere the church is!

Today it is possible, as never before, for Christians from so many different cultures and languages to work effectively together to fulfil the task Jesus gave his disciples. When Christians of different cultures work together in this way it is more difficult for non-Christians to explain away Christian distinctives as only cultural differences. It also helps us to see more clearly in what ways our methods and message really are more a part of our own particular cultural trappings, rather than uniquely a result of the gospel at work in us. And, finally, the greater breadth of experience, expertise and resources might enable us to discover better ways of bridging into those cultures as yet 'unreached'.

In light of Jesus' last words before he returned to the Father, and in light of today's realities, it is impossible to say that we have embraced a Mission Lifestyle if we are not significantly involved cross-culturally. The Cross-cultural Involvement Worksheet in Chapter 15 gives a few ideas as to how we can grow in this crucial aspect of mission. Take some time to fill it out.

Is mission for all Christians or just for the rich?

We've already looked at how mission is an activity for the whole people of God. Therefore it is not restricted to the affluent West. There is a common misconception that those involved in mission are from the affluent part of the world. This is far from the reality of what is happening today.

The early mission workers were not European but from the Middle East, Asia and Africa. It was only later that Europeans joined in. The last twenty-five years have seen a phenomenal growth of missionaries and mission agencies from non-Western countries in Asia, Africa, Latin America and Oceania. There are an estimated 50,000 Protestant missionaries working in over 118 countries of the world. The top ten sending countries of the non-Western world rank India as number one, followed by Nigeria, the Democratic Republic of Congo and Burma.

This shift in reliance on Western missionaries is also happening in parts of Europe. Nations who until recently were receiving missionaries are now beginning to send them.

Zefjan is a young Albanian leader who was converted by missionaries shortly after the fall of communism. As he grew in his faith he began to take on leadership responsibilities. He attended the European Mission Congress in December 1998 with a small group of Albanians.

'The congress challenged and changed our idea of mission. It helped us realise that we Albanians have a part to play,' Zefjan wrote to the organisers. Within three months of returning home, the delegates were involved in mission to Kosovan–Albanian refugees. Some of the group have gone on to be active in church planting and relief work in Kosovo.

Mission is for every believer. There are no financial restrictions.

Where are you?

How are you joining in with the rest of God's people as we fulfil the mission Jesus has given us?

How involved in a local community of Christians are you? How active are you in witnessing among your peers? How involved are you with people of other cultures in your local setting? And how can you be more involved globally?

Is your witness in your present context such that people are asking what it is that makes you different from people who don't follow Jesus? Are you working with other Christians to reach out to people from other cultures who have been brought by God to your doorstep?

Are you trying to understand how God is working through his people in other parts of the world? Are you reading about these brothers and sisters, attempting to communicate with them, visiting them, supporting them?

Are you concerned about those parts of the world where there are few or no churches? Are you doing anything about peoples who have heard little or nothing of the gospel?

Are you confident that you are where God wants you to be and doing what he wants you to be doing? Is he perhaps asking you to be more cross-culturally involved where you are? Or is he even challenging you to travel somewhere you have never been before in order to learn more, or perhaps even calling you to move to a new location and to serve him in new ways?

When the church is not being a clear witness in its immediate context it is failing. When it is not actively pursuing the furtherance of the gospel beyond its own locality, even to the ends of the earth, it is failing.

For the church not to fail, each and every one of us needs to take a good hard look at whether we are where God would have us, and whether we are doing what he wants us to do. God has sent his people to all peoples of the world so that his people will some day include all peoples of the world.

Now that we have looked at the big picture, let us move on to answer the question, 'So where do I fit in?'

4

So Where Do I Fit In?

Helen came to Christ through the witness of a Filipino missionary while at the University of Mindanao. Her priorities changed and she began serving the urban poor in Manila. A few years later God called her to be part of a pioneer team in Vietnam. After two years of intense cross-cultural learning, she returned to the Philippines and helped to lead her organisation through a difficult period of change. Now she is about to finish three years of service in Austria, during which her perspective and experience have significantly influenced and enriched the lives of young people there. Her involvement in Vietnam and Europe has helped to raise the profile of mission, local and global, in her home church in the Philippines.

Judy is a Canadian working with refugees in Australia. Bronnie, an Australian Christian, was challenged by Judy to get involved. Through Bronnie, a Turkish woman, Revnek, came to faith in Christ. Judy is helping to disciple Revnek, who has begun sharing her faith with family and friends back in Turkey.

It is obvious that Judy and Helen are involved in mission, but what about Bronnie, Revnek, the person who led Helen to Christ and the churches in the background of these stories? Are they not also playing a significant role in mission?

It should be becoming clear by now that there is more to mission than just the work of missionaries who go to foreign lands. Our role in mission can perhaps best be described as *God's people making Jesus Christ known to the people of the world*.

Scripture is permeated with stories that make up the overarching story of God calling a people to himself and giving this people the mission of being a blessing to all. He justifies and transforms this people so that it will be an example of what he desires to do with all peoples, indeed with all creation, and also the means through which he accomplishes his plans (Rom. 8:28–30). In other words, he forms what David Bosch calls a 'covenant community' to be both sign and sacrament of the hope which he offers to a hopeless world. This is a community in which, through the indwelling of the Holy Spirit, lives are being transformed, and from which transformational power is overflowing into the surrounding society. This causes those outside the community to ask what it is that makes this group of people so different, and then the basis of our faith, hope and love is clearly explained.

The people of God are to live out the hope of the gospel, allowing others to catch a glimpse and get a foretaste of what God is working towards. Indwelt by the Spirit of God, we are to be a change agent in this broken world, by experiencing and extending his offer of reconciliation, healing, peace, justice and truth. We are to show the world that even in the midst of death there is the hope of resurrection in Christ Jesus. We are to be a reflection of the coming, ultimate revelation of the reign of God, a living prayer that God's will be done on earth as it is in heaven.

Who does the sending?

From what we have discovered so far from our assess-
ment of Scripture, it is the God of Abraham, Isaac and
Jacob throughout the Old Testament and Jesus, the Son of
God in the New Testament, who do the sending. Yet after
Christ's ascension in Acts 1 there is a subtle shift as the
community of believers, the church, becomes not only the
channel, supporter and vehicle for sending, but also the
one sent.

This idea of being both the sender and sent is not an
easy one to maintain, as we much prefer to be either one or
the other. Sometimes even our practice of mission in Western
Europe is not modelled on this duality: often we view mission and the local church as separate and operate accordingly. As a result, in some quarters today we are in danger
of losing sight of this dualism. Some local church leaders
are exasperated by parachurch mission agency demands
for finance and people. Meanwhile, mission agency leaders are frustrated and feel that at times they are outside of
the church. A growing trend for local churches is to so
localise mission that they form their own cross-cultural
mission agencies by making direct contact with local
churches in other cultures. While on many levels this is an
encouraging trend, one disturbing fact is emerging: they
are making exactly the same mistakes in cross-cultural
communication and mission that mission agencies have
already made. Here is one area where mission agencies
and local churches could assist and partner each other.

We have already looked at the different types of global
mission today and how this is a result of a changed world.
Similarly, we need now to see a change in sender and sent
perception and thought so that once again we can hold in
tension the dualism that it is the church, commissioned by
God, who is sent and the sender.

The sending of Barnabas and Saul in Acts 13:1–5 is a classic example of the ideal we should be striving for in local churches today. Here, during a time of prayer and fasting, the Holy Spirit spoke powerfully to all those present, the leaders of a successful local church, to 'set aside' Barnabas and Saul; to commission them and to send them out in cross-cultural mission.

As Antioch was a centre of culture and communication for the Roman Empire, and so had other cultures present, it is highly likely that the local believers were already involved in some form of cross-cultural witness. A look at the make-up of the leaders mentioned in Acts 13:1 further supports the idea that the church in Antioch was culturally mixed. Besides the Palestinians Barnabas, Saul and Manaen, also named are Simeon called Niger, who was possibly of African descent, and Lucius of Cyrene, which today is a port city in Libya.

When considering this scene of local church leaders in prayer and the Holy Spirit speaking to them about cross-cultural mission across geographical borders, it should be remembered that it was not just Barnabas and Saul who were heading out on an adventure. The leaders of the local Christian community were also being called and commissioned to continue and develop the ministry in Antioch. Change was on its way not only for the two leaders they were loosing, but also for the remaining leaders as they stepped up to take on further and perhaps new responsibilities.

Finally, it should be noted that this successful and thriving local church was giving, out of its abundance, its best and most experienced leaders. Barnabas was an Apostle who commended great respect and integrity from not only the community of believers in Antioch, but also in Jerusalem. He had first been sent to Antioch by the leadership and disciples in Jerusalem some years before to encourage and disciple believers (Acts 11:22). Later he went and found Saul and brought him to Antioch to assist him (Acts 11:25–26). Now they were being commissioned together to go and establish the boundaries of the King- dom of God in another place. I have no doubt that if a local church were to face the same situation today, the members would probably insist that one should stay, not both go! However, what we can clearly see here is that the leaders were united with Barnabas and Saul in their calling and discerning of the Holy Spirit's directions.

What are we sent to do?

Jesus tells his followers in Acts 1:8 that they are to be his 'witnesses'. A witness is one who bears testimony to a per- son, place or event in order to establish truth. Under Jew- ish law, at least two witnesses were needed in legal settings to establish truth (Deut. 19:15). This sense of establishing truth was carried forward into the New Tes- tament, where increasingly the word came to encompass not only verbal testimony but also lifestyle and character integrity. When Jesus came to use the word in Acts 1:8, he was requesting his followers to be witnesses for him not only through proclamation but also in the way they con- ducted themselves towards each other and outsiders.

Throughout church history it is this link between ver- bal and non-verbal witnessing that has been difficult to grasp and maintain in balance. Some even today see wit- ness as purely evangelistic verbal proclamation. Others claim that we are to be a witness only through how we live. When these positions are seen as mutually exclusive, the New Testament call is lost. What the New Testament describes as witness is word and deed together. When we attempt to live out our faith without explaining it,

something is lacking from our witness. The same is true
when we proclaim our faith without allowing people to
see life and action that is consistent with it. Peter captures
this dynamic:

> But in your hearts set apart Christ as Lord. Always be pre-
> pared to give an answer to everyone who asks you to give the
> reason for the hope that you have. But do this with gentleness
> and respect, keeping a clear conscience, so that those who
> speak maliciously against your good behaviour in Christ
> may be ashamed of their slander (1 Pet. 3:15–16).

There are three aspects that need to be emphasised.
Firstly, effective witnesses find themselves passionately
involved with the case they seek to present. Like our first-
century predecessors often we cannot but speak of what
we have seen, heard and learnt about Jesus.

Secondly, witnesses are held accountable for the truth-
fulness of their words and actions. Therefore we must
make the effort to get to know Scripture better because,
firstly, it is here that the primary witness to the gospel is
found and, secondly, Scripture lays out the expectations
and principles which guide us in living lives and speaking
words of effective, consistent witness.

Thirdly, witnesses are to be faithful not only to facts of
the Christian message through words and deeds, but also
to their personal meaning, challenge and the changes they
bring. In other words, we are witnesses not only with our
words and deeds, but also our personalities and tempera-
ments – our whole beings and our whole lives are
witnesses.

Therefore we are sent as witnesses to our families and
friends, local communities and world to share, live and be
an example to Jesus. In Luke 4:18–19 Jesus suggests three
ways in which his witness is practical and active:

1 Being able to communicate the gospel in a way people can understand.
2 Caring for those in need.
3 Working to free the oppressed, persecuted and dispossessed.

Where are we sent?

We are sent into the world. To the nations, all nations, even our own! It is not the crossing of ethno-linguistic or geographic boundaries that defines the difference between what is mission and what is not. We have to do that all the time within the wonderful cultural mosaic of the church anyway! No, as we have seen earlier, mission consists of bridging a far more significant gap: the gulf between those who are the people of God and those who are not. When the church is what God intends it to be there is no greater cross-cultural step than this.

Humans are social beings and build elaborate community structures. We might not agree with the way some communities or nations function, they might not be democratic enough, or might not share our Judeo-Christian ethic. Even so, Scripture clearly tells us to go and permeate communities at every level and to be salt, light and yeast. At one of the European Mission Congresses held in the Netherlands, one of the translators received a call from God to be a politician in his home parliament. Shortly after the congress he stood for election, won, and from this position is able to witness to leading politicians across Europe. He's a now missionary to this 'people group'.

David in Psalm 139 writes of being known by God as he was formed in his mother's womb. In the same way, God knows us and has placed us accordingly in the situations and relationships we are in because he wants us to be

witnesses there. He wants us to pray, speak, act and be
'salt and light' in our particular situation. The first place
God sends us, then, is to our own culture, family, friends
and community.

However, 'nothing lasts forever', as my grandmother
was fond of saying at the end of each growing season,
even as she prepared her garden for the next. We need to
be asking regularly, 'Is this still the place where God wants
to use me?' and, if it is, 'Am I sure God wants to keep using
me in the same way here?'

When we are in our own communities, answering this
type of question can be difficult. In secularised, privatised,
pluralised Europe, for example, the great danger to those
who follow Jesus is not overt persecution from society, but
rather a subtle seduction by its values. Subtle seduction
leads to compromise. Speaker and author Tony Campolo
suggests 'Compromise with the culture has always had
more potential for annihilating true faith than has intellec-
tual scepticism or the threat of being thrown to the lions.'

Familiarity can sometimes cloud our vision. It is amazing the difference a little distance can make in perception.
Getting out of your own culture for a time and experiencing situations that are different from what you have
grown accustomed to can help you to understand your
own culture and context better as you see it from new perspectives. This is what Hannes from Austria experienced
last year when he took part in a short-term ministry trip to
the Philippines. His time spent helping with ministries
among the urban poor caused him to view money and
possessions in a completely new way. Since returning he is
attempting to live by a different set of priorities. This, in
turn, has made a difference in his youth group, which has
made several donations in the past year to Filipinos working among the urban poor of Manila and to others moving
to Thailand to begin a new youth ministry.

The experience of leaving your culture and entering another to serve, even for a short time, can be very beneficial. Many who have done this tell of how, upon their return, they have become more aware of and sensitive towards people of other cultures living near them. Some sense God's call to reach out to people they barely even noticed before.

A short-term involvement in another culture can bring you more in tune with what God is doing in other parts of the world as well. Through such an experience, many have been led by God to leave their home context and serve elsewhere. But there is a great need for many, many more Christians to take this step. Such involvement in mission enhances the multi-cultural, global community that is the church, while the accompanying sharing of perspectives, resources and experience improves its local witness. And, finally, if those people in this world who are still isolated from clear Christian witness are to hear the gospel and see its outworking, someone needs to go to them.

Here are the facts of the matter: God sends his people into the entire world. Each Christian is sent into specific contexts to witness. God has placed us in a family, neighbourhood, school or job. God has placed us in proximity to people of other cultures, colours and creeds. God has also placed us in a global setting. This is where we fit in.

If you're a member of the people of God, then global mission is everyone to everywhere; into every culture; to every level of community.

Part II

Mission Lifestyle For The Church

Introduction

Andrew Murray's book *The Key to the Missionary Problem* was first published in 1901 and caused quite a stir around the evangelical world of its day. The *South African Dictionary of National Biography* says that it was no ordinary publication but an 'event in the history of the Christian Church'. The article goes on to suggest that the book had such an impact because Murray 'had a knack, more than any other writer, to place his finger on the salient point or final issue, and bring it to the notice of the world'.[1]

It is this very knack which makes it urgent that Murray's book be read and heard by this generation, for Murray is concerned that the local church be actively and absolutely consumed with the understanding of and participation in global mission. Andrew Murray was himself a local church leader and therefore wanted to address the question of how the local church can be mobilised for such participation. Like today, few were really grappling with these issues in his time, because global mission was viewed as the domain of the mission agency.

Leona Choy, Andrew Murray's biographer, explains how:

---

[1] Leona Choy, *Andrew Murray: Apostle of Abiding Love* (Christian Literature Crusade, 1978), p. 195.

this little volume exploded upon the churches in America, Europe and South Africa in a way that perhaps a spoken message ... even by Murray, could not have done. As a result we have in a more permanent form the summons to global mission involvement as burning and contemporary as it was back in 1901.[2]

The book is based upon four principles, which neatly coincide with our current discussion and understanding of a Mission Lifestyle. The four principles are:

- Firstly, that global mission is the calling upon the whole church and is the primary focus of the church's existence.
- Secondly, the chief end of church leadership and ministry is to guide the church in this calling and ensure she is fit for it.
- Thirdly, preaching and teaching in the church should point to all believers taking up daily and hourly the calling to be living witnesses throughout all of the world in order that the church will fulfil her destiny.
- Finally, each church leader should personally seek the grace of Christ to achieve this work and responsibility of leadership.

For Andrew Murray the challenge of global mission is a personal one for every believer where he or she is to be a living witness. This lesson, suggests Murray, is to be lived and issued by local church leaders because they are called to office under the Great Commission and so therefore have responsibility for mentoring and involving themselves and the people they lead. Therefore, for Murray, a Mission Lifestyle was to be adopted by the church not because it was the latest trend or craze but because it was her destiny and calling from God.

---

[2] Ibid., p. 199.

Contained here is an abridged and contemporised version of Andrew Murray's thoughts, reasoning and challenge to the church of his day. I trust you will sense the same destiny and calling on this generation today and put into action Murray's recommendations, which are based upon Scripture, his own experience and history.

5

Responses To The Ecumenical Missionary Conference

Introduction

One of the gifts we all have is hindsight! As we look back on history we can see how things have worked out and how events and situations develop through time. We are, after all, products of history. This is also true for global mission, and where this is today is a result of the work of those who have gone before us. We are picking up and either spending or investing in the inheritance our Christian forebears have left us. One of the jewels we have in our inheritance is the work of Andrew Murray in response to the Ecumenical Missionary Conference of 1900.

The Ecumenical Missionary Conference

As you will read, because of war in South Africa, Andrew Murray was prevented from attending and speaking at the Ecumenical Missionary Conference. The conference ran from 21 April to 1 May 1900 in New York and was attended by approaching 200,000 people and over 400 mission agencies, making it the largest Christian conference of its day.

It should be noted that the term 'ecumenical' has changed its meaning over the last 100 years or so. Today we would probably use the word 'interdenominational' to describe such a global gathering. The conference was clearly evangelical.

The conference was chaired by Benjamin Harrison, a former President of the United States, and also Theodore Roosevelt, who went on to become President. From the outset it is clear that the speakers at the conference were drawn from a wide perspective and church tradition. It was one of first times that women's ministry was highlighted at a mission conference in such a prominent way. The conference was a forerunner of and paved the way for the 1910 World Missionary Conference in Edinburgh.

Andrew Murray's approach

Even though he was not in attendance, you will notice throughout Murray's response the personal honesty and openness with which he writes. He is both subjective and objective about the conference and himself. This tells us a lot about Andrew Murray the Christian leader. He appears to be a man not only secure in his relationship with God and other leaders, but also one who is dependant upon Jesus and respects Jesus in others. I have found personally refreshing the way he considers the invitation to attend the conference. Here is a prominent church leader questioning himself and God about whether he has a message and what that message should be. I think you will agree that he writes throughout with great humility, integrity and honesty.

As you read the opening words of Andrew Murray, look for:

- Signs of his dependence on God and characteristics not only of his leadership but also spirituality.
- What we can learn from this part of our rich inheritance.

* * * * *

Responses to the Missionary Conference

It was my privilege to be invited to speak at the great Ecumenical Missionary Conference held at New York in April 1900. The circumstances of our country, South Africa, in which war had just broken out, were such that I did not feel at liberty to leave. An urgent letter from D.L. Moody pressing me to come and stay over after the conference for the Northfield gatherings reopened the question. But I was still kept from going.

The invitation, however, gave occasion to much thought and prayer. Did I have a message for that meeting? Would I be able to deliver that message so clearly as to make it worthwhile to go all that distance? Would it be possible amid the great variety of subjects to secure quiet, time and undivided attention for that which appeared to me the one thing needed?

In the midst of such questions, the thought that had long occupied my mind became clearer. I felt that the one point on which I would have wished to speak was this: how could the church be aroused to know and to do our Lord's will for the salvation of humankind?

I had read with much interest the volume that had been issued in preparation for the conference. I had received the impression that while very naturally the chief attention was directed to the active work of mission, locally based work, in preparing the church for doing her part faithfully, hardly had the place its importance demands. There is no greater spiritual and mysterious truth than that Christ our head is actually and entirely dependent upon the members of his Body for carrying out the plans that he, as head, has formed. Only a spiritual person and a church in which spiritual people have influence are capable of rightly carrying out Christ's commands. The clearest argument, the most forcible appeals, result in very little where this is not understood and aimed at as the true standard of Christian devotion.

I feel very deeply that the most important question is: how can we lead the whole church to make herself available to the Lord for the work to which he has destined her and depends on her?

In the preliminary report the subject was hardly alluded to. When I received the two volumes of the report of the conference I naturally turned at once to see how far and in what way the question had been dealt with. I found many important suggestions as to how interest in global mission may be increased. But, if I may venture to say, the root evil, the real cause of so much lack of interest, and the way in which that problem could be met, was hardly dealt with. Indirectly it was admitted that there was something wrong with the greater part of professing Christians. But the real seriousness and sinfulness of the neglect of our Lord's command, indicated by a low state of Christian living, and the problem as to what the mission agencies could do to change the situation certainly did not take that prominent place which I think they deserve.

The following three headings will, I think, be found to cover all that was said in reference to rousing of the church to carry out her Lord's command.

The church leader and the pulpit

Of the suggestions made for putting global mission in its proper place in the work of the church, and in the heart of believers, the first dealt with the church leader and the pulpit. In an address on 'The Church Leader in Relation to the Foreign Field', Dr George F. Pentecost[1] opened with these words:

> To the church leader belongs the privilege and the responsibility of solving the problem of mission. Until the church leaders of our churches wake up to the truth of this proposition, and the global mission becomes a passion in their own hearts and consciences, our mission agencies may do what they can, by way of devising forward movements or organising new methods for raising money from the churches, yet the chariot wheels of global mission will drive heavily.
>
> Every church leader holds office under Christ's commission, and can only fulfil it when he or she counts the whole world as the fold. The church leader of the smallest church has the power to make his or her influence felt around the world. No church leader is worthy of his or her office who does not put him or herself into sympathy with the magnificent breadth of the great commission, and draw inspiration and zeal from its world-wide sweep.
>
> The church leader is not only the instructor but also the leader of a congregation. He or she must not only care for the souls, but direct their activities. If there are churches that do not give and do not pray for global mission, it is because they have church leaders who are falling short of the command of

---

[1] Dr George F. Pentecost was a well-known church leader. Between February 1866 and December 1868 he was the pastor of First Baptist Church, Evansville, Indiana. On 23 September 1874 the *Daily Telegraph*, a leading British newspaper, told how while in England he had an opportunity to preach in the church where Charles Spurgeon was pastor. In his sermon, Pentecost mentioned the struggles he had had quitting smoking and how he believed smoking to be a sin. It was reported that Spurgeon, who was an active cigar smoker, rose afterwards and told his congregation that smoking was no sin!

Christ. I feel almost warranted in saying that, as no congregation can long resist the enthusiastic church leader, so, on the
other hand, a congregation can hardly rise above cold indifference or lack of conviction regarding global mission on the
part of the church leader.

Dr Cuthbert Hall[2] said:

The passion of a Christ-like love for people develops in a
Christian disciple from the presence of powers and activities
that reflect the mind of Christ. And what was the mind of
Christ? A clear vision of what the world is and needs; a deep
feeling of compassion towards the world; active effort for the
world, even to giving his life a ransom for many. The minister
of Christ may speak with the tongues of humans and of
angels, may have all knowledge, may have a faith that could
remove mountains, but if he or she does not have the passion
of a Christ-like love, he or she does not have the Spirit of
Christ.

The problem of the theological seminary is this: not how to
train an occasional individual for work in cross-cultural mission, but how to kindle a global mission passion in every person who passes through the school, that that person may
thereby become an able minister of Christ.

For those who shall enter the church leadership at home,
they must have a global mission passion to make them great
in understanding and apostolic in their view of Christ and
Christianity. To overcome the resistance of ignorance and
prejudice, to awaken the attention of apathetic minds
blinded to the large question of the world's evangelisation, to
educate the church's intelligence, to raise at home the supplies that shall maintain the work of God in global mission,
the church leader needs nothing less than a global mission

---

[2] Dr Cuthbert Hall was a prominent leader in the Young Men's
Christian Association (YMCA) in America.

passion. But those who are thus to conquer must first themselves be conquered and set on fire by God. Personal consecration for personal service is a concept of living that grows more and more attractive to many of our finest minds.

Out of this class of minds shall come the ministry of the future:

- It shall be a Christ-filled ministry, beholding the glory of God in the face of Jesus Christ, worshipping him with the enthusiasm of an absolutely fearless affection, and presenting him as the only name under heaven whereby people can be saved.
- It shall be a global-mission-worker-focused ministry, full of passion to redeem, clear-eyed to discover the ongoing of Christ's work, faithful in its stewardship in all places across the globe.
- It shall be apostolic in its assurance that Christ has ordained it to bear much fruit; apostolic in its eagerness to spread far and wide the gospel of the risen and ascended Lord; and apostolic in its hope that the unseen and crowned Saviour shall surely come again.

Another prominent church leader, Revd D.S. MacKay, called attention to the church leader's work:

A special appeal, to be effective, must have not only behind it, but in it, pulsating through it, the persuasive personality of the local church leader. To scatter a few leaflets in the pews, and simply call attention to them, is one of the surest ways by which a church leader can kill a special appeal. The effectiveness of the appeal depends, in the last instance, on the church leader who with loving zeal drives home the appeal. I do not denigrate in any way the helpfulness of missionaries from time to time in our pulpits, but it is the faithfulness of the local church leader, translating the special appeal into an individual message to his or her own people, that is, after all, the secret of success in global mission.

Will an emphasis on global mission detract from concern for the local church and community? On the contrary! Bishop Hendrix of the Church of England gave a concrete illustration:

> Andrew Fuller, alarmed at the spiritual indifference of his church, preached a sermon on the duty of the church to give the gospel to the world; and as he broadened their intellectual understanding, and stirred their zeal and their purpose, he followed it up the next Sunday with another sermon on the duty of the church to give the gospel to the world. The third Sunday the same theme was presented from his pulpit. Then people began to enquire: 'If the gospel can save the world, can it also save our own children, our own community?' And from that missionary sermon sprang one of the most memorable revivals in the history of any church.

It is one thing for ministers to be advocates and supporters of global mission; it is another and very different thing for them to understand that mission is the chief end of the church and therefore the chief end for which their congregation exists. It is only when this truth masters them in its spiritual power that they will be able to give the subject of global mission its true place in their ministry. They must see how every believer is called to witness to Christ's love and claim, and how healthy spiritual life depends on the share the believer takes in work for his or her Lord. They must learn how to lead the congregation on to make the extension of Christ's Kingdom the highest object of its corporate existence.

In order to carry this out, the essential power lies in a definite consecration to be filled with the Spirit and the love of Christ. As they think of all the ignorance and worldliness and unbelief that they have to contend with, they will learn that their enthusiasm for global mission must not be of the flesh but the enthusiasm of the Holy

Spirit. They will then be filled with an intense love for Christ, an intense faith in his power, an intense desire to lead all his disciples to give their lives to make Jesus King over the whole earth.

The more earnestly we study global mission in the light of the church leaders' responsibility, the more we shall see that everything depends upon the personal life being wholly under the power of love for Christ, as the constraining power of our work. With the church leader, at least, it will be found that the problem of global mission is a personal one.

The pen and the press

Next to the influence of the church leader and the pulpit in arousing interest in global mission, the second place was given to the pen and the press.[3] The need of preparing, circulating and securing the study of mission literature was forcibly put from various points of view. The following paragraphs summarise the thoughts of various speakers.

Information is the fuel without which the fire cannot burn. Fuel is not fire, and cannot of itself create fire; but where there is fire, fuel is indispensable to keep it burning, or to make it burn with greater intensity. An informed church will be a transformed church. Possibly one of the greatest factors in the development of interest in global mission is the systematic study of mission.

The influence of global mission literature is twofold.

Firstly, the torch we hold up for others illuminates our own path. The church is watching and working and

---

[3] Today we would also include the use of the video or DVD, cassette tape and the Internet. However, the principles and issues raised in 1900 are unfortunately transferable to the other media we now have at our disposal.

praying people to become Christians.[4] Our representatives are out in the thickest of the battle. It is a struggle
between the forces of life and death. Are we so swathed in
our small environment that we do not care for news of this
contest with the forces of darkness? If we are in earnest to
plant the church of Christ in the ends of the earth, let us
hear the report of progress and pass it on. Ignorance is the
source of weakness in missionary effort. Know, and you
will believe. Know, and you will pray. Know, and you will
help in the front rank.

Secondly, another speaker pointed to the direction for our
attitude:

> With such a spirit of nature, with wonder, with reverence,
> with humility must the church leader approach the study of
> global mission literature. As you study the literature of mis-
> sion, the conviction will deepen that though you are reading
> about the lives of Christians of many denominations and var-
> ied attainments, engaged in a great variety of work in differ-
> ent lands, yet the one fact that confronts you is that these
> missionaries believe in the presence of the Spirit of God! The
> church leader who neglects such literature robs people of
> their birthright and wrongs his or her own soul.

The people and the pew

The third great means of awakening interest was that of
personal influence exercised through church-related

---

[4] This is still the case. During the 1990s there were an estimated
thirty million believers taking part in the prayer initiative
Praying Through the 10/40 Window; the increasing sales of
book *Operation World* by Patrick Johnstone and Jason Mandryk
(Paternoster, 2001); and one of the most visited parts of the
www.mission.org web site is the Harvest Hands prayer area.
All point to a growing interest in global mission.

organisations. There is great importance in having children, young people, men, women, all separately gathered under the influence of leaders who can expertly guide their training for the love and service of the Kingdom. We must gratefully acknowledge the power teachers are already exercising, and must exercise still more largely, in receiving and passing on the wonderful love of Jesus Christ within the local churches, to train and prepare the future church for giving herself to the work of global mission.

Mrs T. B. Hargrove[5] made very plain the importance of youth workers:

> The church is truly thinking the thoughts of Christ after him when she recognises the importance of the child in the development of his Kingdom on earth. The youth groups of the church are just like training schools where the workers of the future are being prepared to take the places of the veterans of today.
>
> Shall we not take care of the lambs by keeping both children and youth groups under the care of 'good shepherds'? They must have our very best; if a choice must be made for a superior leader between the adults or the youth work, always give the young people the preference.
>
> Each youth worker should make it his or her first aim to inspire in every young person a real love for Christ and for the unbeliever. Perhaps the discipling of the young in their homes, in the schools and groups, is more defective just here than in any other one point.

There is a great deal more of much value in connection with organisation that took place at the conference that I

---

[5] Mrs T.B. Hargrove was one of many women to address the conference. Many of the women speakers present went on to partner together in fostering prayer for global mission, an expression of which today is the continuance of the World Day of Prayer on the last Friday of March each year.

cannot refer to here. What I have quoted is enough to show how much will have to be done before the church has fully availed herself of this wonderful power.

In summary, if our church leaders are brought to believe that the great aim of the existence of their congregations is to make Christ known to every creature; if our people would read and take an interest in the news of the Kingdom and its extension; if we could so get our Christian men and women of devotion to organise our young people so that their training in mission service were part of their education in the love of Christ and the life of godliness; if our students could be trained in an atmosphere of global mission enthusiasm, there would be reason to hope that the work will be accomplished. Within thirty years every man and woman in the world would have the gospel brought within their reach, and actually offered to them.

Yet throughout all the addresses there is the secret admission that in all these respects there is reason for anxiety. Complaints were voiced about the lack of the ideal and passion of global mission in many church leaders and students, and the lack of interest by the majority of church members in mission literature. Many, many more are needed to shepherd the young into the life of developing a Mission Lifestyle. These issues prove that behind all these needs is a deeper need: there is need of a great spiritual awakening of spiritual life, of truly fervent devotion to our Lord Jesus, of entire consecration to his service. It is only in a church in which this spirit of awakening has at least begun that there is any hope of any very radical change in the relation of the majority of our Christian people to the work of global mission.

I had hoped that this question, as the one of paramount importance in view of the possibility of carrying out Christ's command at once, would have absorbed the attention of the conference. When the Student Volunteer Movement[6] issued its appeal to the churches, announcing the motto it had adopted, 'The evangelisation of the world in this generation',[7] its message met with a most enthusiastic welcome and response. Must we now wait for Jesus to come a second time and ask the church what the great hindrance is that holds his people back from meeting the emergency with the enthusiasm that he has a right to claim? Is it time for us to enquire of ourselves into the nature and extent of the disease that is so paralysing the church? At the same time we need to know the conditions for restoration to health and strength. To know what is wrong, and with confession and humility to turn from it to the loving Lord, will bring new life to the church and altogether new power for the work that has to be done.

It is under the spiritual burden of such thoughts that I felt led to write this book. I know that it is no easy task to speak humbly, wisely, lovingly, and yet faithfully and effectually, of what appears lacking or sinful in the church. And yet I am sure that there are many who would welcome help in answering the questions:

- Is there any real possibility of such a spiritual awakening in the church that in every congregation where the

---

[6] The Student Volunteer Movement (1888–1969) was a North American organisation dedicated to mobilising students into global mission. During its life some 20,000 young people dedicated themselves to actively participate in global mission as mission workers.

[7] When this phrase was used at the conference and by Murray it was meant to stress the responsibility each Christian generation has to witness to its generation. It was not meant to be a prophecy whereby Christ's return was wholly dependant on the proclamation of the gospel. Rather it was a rallying call to push witness into today's world.

full gospel is preached her most important aim will be to carry the gospel to every creature?
- What is the path that will lead to this change?
- What steps should be taken by those who currently lead the global mission of the church?

May God by his Holy Spirit guide us to the vision of his will concerning his church, to the faith in his power and promise, and to the obedience that will walk in any path he opens up.

6

Mission – A Test of the State of the Church

Introduction

Local churches come in all shapes, sizes and varieties! There are those with thousands in membership or those with just a handful in the congregation; those that meet in purpose-built premises; and those that meet in community centres, homes, schools, or in the open air. Some belong to denominations, others don't. Worship differs: some like to sing; others can't because if they were heard it could bring persecution. Worship styles are different too, from 'charismatic' to liturgical. Some welcome young people and enjoy having them around; others frown upon them.

Whatever type of local church we belong to and wherever the church is, there are two points that unite us. The first is our eagerness to criticise the church and its leadership. As I have travelled and visited churches many young Christian people have moaned to me and said how boring the church is. I have often pointed out they should remember that if they are a Christian then they are part of the church, and as part of the church they are calling themselves boring! Are they then therefore admitting they are part of the problem?

Secondly, we are all part of the Body of Christ, the church – yesterday, today and tomorrow. Therefore we need to take our eyes off ourselves in our little corner and look around us to the global and universal church that Christ is building. Whatever the variety, whatever the brand, whatever the nationality, it's the church that Jesus said he would build and 'the power of death will not be able to defeat it' (Matt. 16:18). In countries like Sudan and Iran Christians are facing persecution because of their faith, yet the church is growing. One Sudanese church leader told me recently to ask the West to pray for the persecution to continue and not stop because while it continued more and more people were becoming Christians and were willing to talk about their faith.

In this next chapter of Andrew Murray you will notice how he not only endorses the criticism made by speakers at the conference, but also sounds a warning that they are dealing with and talking about the Body of Christ. Murray has a high regard for the church; he was after all first and foremost a local church leader. Therefore, when he endorses the criticism made of the local church, he was also examining his own ministry in South Africa.

As you study this chapter:

- Allow the charges made of the church to be levelled at you personally.
- Examine your local church situation and ask if the same situation applies today.
- Search your heart and motive for any negative criticism you have made against the church.

* * * * *

Mission – A Test of the State of the Church

In the previous chapter I raised the question of what can be done to so stimulate the spiritual life of the church that global mission shall have all the hearty enthusiasm and support it deserves? To answer that question we must first form an accurate appraisal of the real relationship of the church to global mission work.

In this chapter we will consider the state of the church. As the basis of our study, we will take passages from addresses given at the conference. The frequent use of the word '*if*' points to how the church has failed in her duty and suggests the state in which she should and could be found. Moreover, we must ask the cause of failure, and what cure might be found for such a condition.

Dr John R. Mott[1] emphasised four areas of failure:

1   People and Resources:

The Moravians[2] have done more in proportion to their ability than any other body of Christians. *If* members of Protestant churches in Great Britain and America gave in like proportion, contributions to global mission would aggregate a fourfold increase. *If* we went out as mission workers in corresponding numbers, we would have a force of nearly 400,000 workers, which is vastly more than the number of missionaries estimated as necessary to achieve the evangelisation of the world in this generation. I ask the question, what has there been in connection with their work which is not reproducible?

---

[1] Dr John R. Mott (1865–1955) was a mission mobiliser in America. He was the co-founder and leader of the Student Volunteer Movement in 1888. Dr Mott's motto was 'With God anywhere, without him, not over the threshold.'

[2] Andrew Murray explains in greater details the background of the Moravian Church later in Chapter 7, 'Love to Christ as Motivation'.

2   Witness:

The world-wide proclamation of the gospel can be accomplished by this generation *if* it has the obedience and determination to attempt the task. There is not a single country on the face of the earth to which the church, *if* she seriously desired, in our time, could not send ambassadors of Christ to proclaim his message.

3   Unity:

Contrast the millions of members in Protestant churches with the few thousand which on the day of Pentecost began the work. As we recall the achievements of that infant church, can we deny the possibility of present-day Christians to give all humankind an opportunity to know Christ, *if* they united to accomplish it?

4   Finance:

The money-power of the church is enormous. *If* only one fourth of the members of Protestant churches gave one penny a day, it would yield over twenty-five million pounds in contrast with the less than four million pounds of the past year.[3]

In his address, Mr Robert Speer[4] similarly declared:

The aim of mission is to make Jesus Christ known to the world. The church could do the work *if* this aim ruled her spirit. I was glad to read ... those dying words of Simeon Calhoun: 'It is my deep conviction, and I say it again and

---

[3] George Verwer in his book *Out of the Comfort Zone* (Carlisle: Paternoster, 2000), p. 24 estimates that there are 35,000 who have committed themselves to cross-cultural mission but 95 per cent of them will not make it because of lack of finance. He goes further and suggests that currently mission has only 10 per cent of what is actually needed.

[4] Mr Robert Speer (1867–1947) was an American mission mobiliser who combined a passion for evangelism and the proclamation of the gospel with a concern for the physical and social needs of people.

again, that *if* the church of Christ were what she ought to be, before twenty years would pass the story of the cross would be proclaimed in the ears of every living man and woman.'

The *ifs* all indicate something wrong in the church in reference to Christ's command to global mission. We all know the force of the word *if*. It suggests a cause from which certain effects can follow. It points to the condition needed to ensure the results we desire. In the passages quoted, and in different forms of expression frequently recurring in mission literature, we find the same thought incessantly repeated:

How certainly and speedily the evangelisation of the world could be accomplished *if* it were not for the failure of the church in doing the part that has been assigned her by God.

Such statements are not important in themselves. More important are the lessons we ought to learn, and what can be done to roll away the reproach resting on us as a church of Christ.

These *ifs* suggest four questions and charges: firstly, is the church really at fault, and how? Secondly, is it possible for her to have actually done what was claimed? Thirdly, what is the cause of the present failure? Fourthly, how is deliverance from this evil to be found?

These charges against the church were not brought by unbelievers or enemies, but by some of the church's most faithful servants. They were spoken in the presence of thousands of mission workers and mission friends. If they were not true they would have been denied and refuted. But no one could deny them. However devotedly a small part of the church is doing its utmost, the great majority of her members are not what they should be. They do not truly desire to make Christ known to every creature as speedily as possible. This aim does not rule the spirit of the church – she is not prepared to do her duty.

The charge is extremely serious and solemn. It is not good enough just to listen and then lay it aside and forget it. Everyone who loves Christ's church, who loves Christ Jesus his or her Lord, who loves the souls that are perishing through this neglect, ought to pause and consider what it means. Christ has given his life in serving us and asked us to give our lives in serving him; Christ has put his dying love into our hearts and asked us to impart it to others; in his love, Christ has died for all, and has made himself dependent on us to let them know of that love; Christ has endured the agony of the cross for the joy of winning and saving the perishing and has counted on our love to delight in making him happy and bringing him his reward.

Yet the great majority of those who profess to owe everything to his dying love are utterly indifferent either as to pleasing him or blessing others by winning them to that love. Surely his love can never have been a reality to them, or they could not so neglect their calling. Can it be that they have never been correctly taught what they have been redeemed for? The church, in calling them to seek salvation for themselves, must have kept hidden from them the great purpose for which they were redeemed – that they should witness to save others.

Whatever the cause, here is the solemn fact:

> A church, purchased by the blood of the Son of God to be his messenger to a dying world, for the greater part has failed entirely to understand and fulfil her calling. No words can express, no mind can grasp, the terrible meaning and consequences of the failure and condemnation involved in the simple *ifs* of which we speak.

And let us not think that this failure is because of some natural impossibility. These *ifs* point to what is the church's actual destiny. Dreamers speak of impossibilities and calculate what might be done if they came true. We are listening to people who are speaking words of soberness and truth. These *ifs* suggest what is certainly and divinely possible. They point us to the church at the time of Pentecost.

The first generation of believers did more to accomplish the work of global mission than has any succeeding generation. In studying the secret of what they accomplished, one is led to the conclusion that they employed no vitally important method which cannot be used today, and that they availed themselves of no power which we cannot utilise.

The mighty power of God and his Holy Spirit are ours as well as theirs. We are heirs to all that the first-century church had at Pentecost:

> The power of his dying love in the heart; a triumphant faith in Christ; simple, bold, personal testimony; patient suffering; absolute passionate consecration; the heavenly power that overcomes the world and makes us more than conquerors through him that loved us.

As was pointed out, the Moravian Church was one of the smallest in number and poorest in means of all the churches. What the Moravian Church has done is proof that the whole church, when she rouses herself to her calling, most surely can accomplish the work. In view of the opportunities the church has in the open doors in every country of the world, of the enormous resources the church possesses in the wealth of her members, in the numbers of workers over which the church has disposal, and the faith that to send them out would, instead of weakening it, bring quickening and strength, it is absolutely within the power of the church to bring the gospel to every creature.

Let us take time to come under the full power of this great thought. It will give force to what has been said about the terrible failure of the church. It will prepare us for discovering how to deal with the evil.

These *ifs* invite us to ask the causes of this shortcoming:

- Why has the church of Christ been so utterly unfaithful?
- Does not our Protestant Christendom profess and honestly acknowledge Christ as its Lord and God's holy Word as the law of its life?
- Is it not our boast that we are in the true succession of the early church, the heirs of all her promises and powers?
- Are we, the church, not in possession of the great truths that everyone has a right to God's Word as taught by God's Spirit, and a free access through Christ to God's pardoning grace?
- Is it not the centre of our profession that we acknowledge Jesus as Master and Lord, and have given ourselves to do what he says?

Then why is it that in the very thing on which Christ's glory most depends, on which his heart of love is most set, the church should have failed to realise or fulfil her destiny?

It would be easy to mention many causes that co-operate in producing this unfaithfulness. But they may all be summed up in the low spiritual state of the church as a whole.

The control of the Holy Spirit in power and fullness over the life of believers is essential to the health and strength of the church. Scripture teaches us how easy it is for a church and its members to have a sound creed, a faithful observance of services and duties, a zeal for the extension of the church and for works of philanthropy which are within the range of human nature, while that which is definitely spiritual, supernatural and divine is to a large extent lacking. The spirit of the world, the wisdom and the will of humanity in the teaching of the Word and the guidance of the church, make it very much like any other human institution. There is little of the power of the heavenly world and eternal life to be seen in her. In such a church mission may still have a place, though not the place nor the power that is needed for fulfilling the command of Christ. The passion of love to Christ and to souls, the enthusiasm of sacrifice for humanity and of faith in the omnipotent power that can quicken the dead is lacking.

Worldliness and lack of prayer are among the chief symptoms of this sickly state. If there is one thing that Christ and Scripture insist on, it is that his Kingdom is not of this world, that the spirit of the world cannot understand the things of God (John 18:36); that separation from the world in fellowship and conduct, in surrender to the Spirit who is from heaven, is essential to the faithful following of the Lord Jesus (Rom. 12:1–2).

The one universally admitted fact – that the majority of Christians care nothing and give nothing for global mission, that a large number give but little and not from the highest motives – is simply a proof of the worldliness in which most Christians live. The world needed Christ to come from heaven to save people. It needs the Spirit of heaven in Christ's disciples to free them from the spirit of the world, to make them willing to sacrifice all to win the world for Christ. It needs the same Spirit, through whom Christ gave his life for the world, to revive his church to win the world for God.

Lack of prayer is another symptom of this sickly state. A worldly spirit in Christians hinders their praying. They look at things in the light of the world. They are not at home in heavenly places. They do not realise the dark power of sin in those around them, or the urgent need of direct divine intervention. They have little faith in the effectiveness of prayer, in the need of much and unceasing prayer, in the power there is in them to pray in Christ's name and win through. True financial support is the giving from devotion to Christ and true prayer is the asking and counting upon him to bless the gift and bestow his Spirit in his work. Both prove that the worldly spirit is being overcome, and that the soul is being restored to spiritual health. *If* the church is to be what she ought to be, and to do what her Lord asks her to do for the evangelisation of the world, this sickness and failure must be acknowledged, and deliverance sought.

Steps back to health

Confess to God

The first step in returning to God for true service and renewed blessing is always confession.

The leaders of mission work ought to know how tremendous are the needs of the world; they should understand the meaning and urgency of our Lord's command; they are to feel the utterly inadequate provision the church is making for his work. On them rests the solemn duty of lifting up their voices and making God's people know their sin. It is possible that we are all so occupied with our special fields of labour and the thought of how much is being done that the extent and guilt of what is not being done is comparatively lost sight of.

Until Christians are led to listen, think and pray for opened eyes to look upon the fields of the ripe harvest entrusted to them, they never will recognise the greatness of the work, their own unpreparedness, or the urgent need of waiting for divine power to fit them for the task (John 4:35).

As we take this in, we shall feel and confess how little the church has done. The guilt and shame resting on Christ will become the Lord's burden on us. We rejoice and give thanks for the 15,460 cross-cultural missionaries who are now in the field labouring among the 4 million in Christian communities.[5] But what efforts are being made to reach the 1,000 million? What prospect is there that they will be speedily reached?

Every mission organisation and agency complains of lack of funds. We are told that of church members one-third neither gives nor cares for the Kingdom; that another third gives but cares very little, and does not give from the right motives; and that even of the remaining third (it is really less than a third) only a small proportion are doing their utmost and giving and praying with their whole heart. The disobedience of the church in the great majority of her members, her neglect of her Lord's work, her refusal to listen to the appeals to come to his help – is not this a sin and a guilt greater than we think?

If the church is really to awaken out of her sleep, the one thing needed is that those to whom God has given the charge of his mission work in the world should lay before the people the utter disproportion between what is being done and what ought to be and can be done. They should press home the guilt and the shame of it until an increasing number bow before God in confession and humility and with a cry for pardon and mercy as earnest as when they sought their own salvation.

---

[5] Today the number of missionaries in cross-cultural activity in their home country or involved in partnering with foreign churches is 516,000. Only 13,200 are ministering among 4.15 billion non-Christians in areas where there is either no or a very small number of believers. Source: World Evangelisation Research Centre (USA), www.gem-werc.org

Appeal to God

With this appeal there must be also an appeal to God. The work is his: he cares for it. The power is his: he gives it. The church is his: he waits to use it. The world is his: he loves it. He can make his people willing in the day of his power. He will hear the cries of his servants who give him no rest. He delights to prove his faithfulness in fulfilling his promises. Things cannot continue as they are if the world is really to be evangelised in this generation. In this generation every person must have the gospel offered to him or her. Unless there is a great change in the church and she give herself to the work in a way she has not yet done the work cannot be accomplished. But it can be accomplished *if* God's people will fall upon their faces before him to confess their sin and the sin of their brethren.

Let them ask God to reveal the cause of all the failure, and then take the message to his church. Let them preach the great truth: that the winning of the world to God is the supreme purpose of the church's existence. The love of souls, the surrender of the whole life to Christ for his use in the winning of souls, is the duty, is the only healthy life, for every believer. There are tens of thousands of God's children who are willing, yes, who are secretly longing to serve their Lord, but don't know how, or don't have the courage to do so.

The time will come when we shall no longer have to say '*If the church were what she ought to be ...* '. We shall find our joy and strength in guiding a prepared people in that arduous but blessed path of bearing Christ's cross to every person on God's earth, and wrestling with the hosts of hell to make way for the Kingdom of Christ the conqueror!

7

Love to Christ as Motivation

Introduction

We are all products of history. This fact is, however, easily overlooked or forgotten because we so often live in the immediate, the now. The playwright and author George Bernard Shaw had this in mind when he said that we learn from history that we learn nothing from history.

In this chapter Andrew Murray uses the real-life events in the history of the Moravian Church to illustrate how the Moravians' life in Christ motivated them to participate in global mission. Murray shares how the history of the Moravian Church and the life of Nicholas Louis von Zinzendorf became so entwined that their devotion to Christ led to blessing around the world. In using this history, Murray draws out important lessons for church leaders and members of local congregations, which are focused on prayer being foundational to global mission participation. However, he does not make prayer an end in itself, but rather a vehicle to hear from God the Father, Son and Holy Spirit as to how, where and when to step out into action.

As you read this chapter, consider:

- What lessons can be learnt personally from the experiences of the Moravian Church?

- What can be learnt about Nicholas Louis von Zinzendorf's style of leadership?
- Also, think through for yourself the depth of your love to Christ and his love to you in light of how much this motivates you for global mission.

* * * * *

Love to Christ as Motivation

At the conference, the Secretary of the Board of Missions of the Moravian Church in the United States, Revd P. de Schweinitz, summed up the work of the church in these words:

> Even today [in 1900] the Moravians have for every fifty-eight communicants in the home churches a missionary in the foreign field, and for every member in the home churches there are more than two members in the congregations where their missionaries labour. What was the incentive for global mission work which has produced such results?
>
> While acknowledging the supreme authority of the Great Commission, the Moravian Church has always emphasised as its chief incentive the inspiring truth from Isaiah 53:10–12, making our Lord's suffering the spur to all activity. From that prophecy the Moravians drew their battlecry: 'To win for the Lamb that was slain, the reward of his sufferings.'
>
> We feel that we must compensate him in some way for the awful sufferings he endured in working out our salvation. The only way we can reward him is by bringing people to faith in him. Whether we go ourselves or enable others to go, in no other way can we so effectively bring the suffering Saviour the reward of his passion. Get this burning thought of 'personal love for the Saviour who redeemed me' into the hearts of all Christians, and you have the most powerful incentive for the global mission effort.

Oh! If we could make the problem of global mission a personal one! If we could fill the hearts of the people with a personal love for the Saviour who died for them, the indifference of Christendom would disappear, and the Kingdom of Christ would appear.

If the example of the Moravians is to exercise any influence and the church world-wide to be aroused to follow in their footsteps, we must find out what the principles were that animated them, where they got the power that enabled them to do so much, and especially how God fitted them for doing that work. We cannot have like effects without like causes. As the conditions of their successes are discovered, the path to restoration for the church today can be found.

A history of the Moravian Church

Their origins

Moravia was, from the eleventh century, a province of the kingdom of Bohemia, which now forms part of the modern-day Czech Republic. In the seventh and eighth centuries this region received knowledge of the gospel first from the Greek church and later from the Roman church. As the former allowed preaching in the national language and gave the people the Bible in their own language, there arose divisions, which were the cause of unceasing conflict. Gradually the Roman church got the upper hand, and from the beginning of the fifteenth century, when John Huss was burned at the stake for preaching the gospel (in 1415), this region was the scene of terrible persecution. In the course of time those who remained faithful to the gospel gathered in a village in the north-east of Bohemia, in the valley of Kunwald, where they were allowed for a time to live in comparative peace. Here, in 1457, they were known as 'The Church of the Law of Christ'. When their church was established, they assumed the name of The United Church.

Their self-discipline

One of the brightest jewels of this church was its members' self-discipline. It was not only their doctrine but their life; not only their theory but their practice that made them such a force to be reckoned with.

When the Reformers later became acquainted with the church, Martin Bucer, the German Protestant Reformer, wrote:

> You alone, in all the world, combine a wholesome discipline with a pure faith. When we compare our Church with yours, we must be ashamed. God preserve to you that which he has given you.

Calvin wrote:

> I congratulate your churches that the Lord, in addition to pure doctrine, has given them so many excellent gifts, and that they maintain such good morals, order, and discipline. We have long since recognised the value of such a system, but cannot in any way attain to it.

Luther said:

> Tell the Church that they should hold fast that which God has given them, and not relinquish their constitution and discipline.

And what was their discipline? In every detail of their lives – in business, in pleasure, in Christian service, in civil duties – they took the Sermon on the Mount as a guiding lamp. They counted the service of God the one thing to live for, and everything was made subservient to this. Their ministers and elders were to keep watch over the flock, to see that all were living to the glory of God. All were to be united in one community, helping and encouraging one another in a quiet and godly life.

Their sufferings and suppression

For some fifty years they lived in Kunwald relatively untroubled, though persecuted elsewhere. At the turn of the sixteenth century, the Pope and the King of Bohemia combined against them. In 1515, just as the Reformation was dawning in Germany, it almost looked as if they would be extinguished. With intervals of toleration, their troubles continued, until in 1548 a Royal Edict drove thousands to Poland, where they established a large and prosperous church. With the accession a new king in 1556, peace returned, and the church was again firmly established and divided into the three provinces of Bohemia, Moravia and Poland. By the end of the century the church had given a Bible to the people, and had fostered education to such a degree that the Bohemian schools had a noted reputation in Europe, the people being considered the best-educated people in the world.

But with the accession of King Frederick II everything suddenly changed. The Day of Blood at Prague in 1620 witnessed the execution of twenty-seven of the leading nobles. During the 6 years that followed, Bohemia was a field of blood, and 36,000 families left the country. The population dwindled from three million to one million and the Church of the United Brethren (as The United Church was now named) was broken up and scattered. During the whole century those who stayed in the country worshipped God in secret, and formed what was called 'The Hidden Seed'.

When we take up the thread again in 1722, just 100 years have elapsed, during which only God knows what was suffered. Yet even during that period hope was not altogether dead.

In 1707 George Jaeschke,[1] one of the few witnesses to the truth at that time, then aged eighty-three, said:

> It may seem as though the final end of the United Brethren Church has come. But, my beloved children, you will see a great deliverance. The remnant will be saved. I do not know whether this deliverance will come to pass here in Moravia, or whether you will have to go out of 'Babylon'; but I do know it will transpire not very long hence. I am inclined to believe that an exodus will take place, and that a refuge will be offered on a spot where you will be able, without fear, to serve the Lord according to his holy Word.

Their place of refuge

The Lord had indeed provided for his people a place of refuge, where the United Brethren would be renewed. It was in 1722 that Christian David received from Count Nicholas Louis von Zinzendorf permission to bring refugees from Moravia to his estate in Saxony. As a soldier in Saxony Christian David found Christ from the teaching of a godly Lutheran church leader. He returned to Moravia to preach the Saviour he had found, and spoke with such power that an awakening followed. Persecution was immediately aroused, and the preacher went to find a refuge for the persecuted. When he had obtained Count Zinzendorf's permission he returned and led out his first band of ten, who reached Berthelsdorf in June 1722.

---

[1] George Jaeschke was the father of Michael Jaeschke, and grandfather of Augustin and Jakob Neisser, who with their wives and children formed the first party led to Hernhutt.

Time after time this devoted servant of the Lord went back to preach the gospel and to lead out those who were willing to forsake all. In this way it was not long before some 200 had gathered, many of them among those who had been called 'The Hidden Seed', the true descendants of the old church. The spot allotted to them had been called Hutberg, 'The Watch Hill'. They called their new settlement Hernhutt, 'The Lord's Watch'. They took the word in its double meaning: the watch of the Lord over them and the watch of the Lord to be kept by them in prayer.

Their new leader

Count Zinzendorf was born in May 1700, of godly parents. On his deathbed his father had taken the child, then only six weeks old, in his arms, and consecrated him to the service of Christ. 'Already in my childhood', wrote Zinzendorf, 'I loved the Saviour, and had abundant communion with Him. In my fourth year I began to seek God earnestly, and determined to become a true servant of Jesus Christ.'

At the Franke's school in Halle, aged twelve, he often met missionaries, and his heart was touched with the thought of work for Christ among the unevangelised. Among the boys at school he founded the 'Order of the Mustard Seed'. They bound themselves to be kind to all people, to seek their welfare, and to try to lead them to God and to Christ. As an emblem, they had a small shield with the motto 'His wounds our healing'. Each member wore a ring, on which was inscribed 'No man liveth unto himself'. Before leaving Halle he entered into a covenant with an intimate friend for the conversion of the unevangelised, especially such as would not be cared for by others.

From Halle he went to Wittenberg University, where he held prayer meetings for the other students, and often spent whole nights in prayer and study of the Bible. It was at about this time that Zinzendorf visited the art gallery in Dusseldorf, where he saw the *Ecce Homo* painting by Steinberg, with the words 'All this I did for thee, What hast thou done for Me?' underneath.

His heart was touched. He felt as if he could not answer that question. He turned away more determined than ever to spend his life in the service of his Lord. The vision of that face never left him. Christ's love became the constraining power of his life. 'I have', he exclaimed, 'but one passion: "Tis He, and He only."' It was his dying love that fitted Christ for the work God had given him as the Saviour of humankind. It was the dying love of Christ mastering his life that fitted Zinzendorf for the work he had to do.

A spiritual awakening in the church

When Zinzendorf settled on his estate, he devoted himself to the spiritual welfare of his tenants. With three like-minded friends he formed the League of the Four Churches. The object was to proclaim to the world the 'universal religion of the Saviour and his family of disciples, the heart-religion in which the Saviour is the central point'. He joined the church leaders of the congregation in preaching, in meetings for prayer and singing. He lived for Christ and the people he had died to save.

In offering the Moravian exiles a refuge on his estate, he had simply thought of giving them a home, in which they should earn their livelihoods and be free in the exercise of their religion. When it was known that Hernhutt was a refuge for the persecuted, all sorts of displaced religious persons came to seek a home there.

The spirit of discord speedily entered, and there was danger of Hernhutt becoming a seat of sectarianism and fanaticism. Zinzendorf felt that the time had come for him to intervene. He had faith in the uprightness and earnestness of the Moravian settlers. He gave himself personally to loving dealings with the leaders.

Many of them had felt deeply the sin and pain of division, and had been praying that, by the grace of God, the spirit of true fellowship might be restored. With many tears and prayers, in the love and patience of Jesus Christ, the Count pleaded with those who were in error. One point on which the Moravians (they were more than 200 out of the 300 that had come to Hernhutt) would not give way was their unwillingness to be absorbed into the Lutheran Church. They insisted on having the discipline of the old Moravian Church maintained. The Count was afraid that this might give rise to prejudice and misunderstanding in the church around them, but he felt that their claim was just, and resolved at any risk to yield to them. The principles and discipline of the old Moravian Church were to be restored. Zinzendorf drew up the Statutes, Injunctions and Prohibitions according to which they were to live.

12 May 1727, just five years after the first arrivals on to his estate, was a memorable day in the history of the church – Zinzendorf called the people together and read to them the Statutes that had been agreed on. There was to be no more discord. The love and unity they found in Christ were to be the golden chains that bound them together. All the members shook hands and pledged themselves to obey the Statutes. That day was the beginning of new life in Hernhutt.

It was recorded:

> This day the Count made a covenant with the Lord. The Church all promised, one by one, that they would be the

Saviour's true followers. Self-will, self-love, disobedience – they bade these farewell. They would seek to be poor in spirit; no one was to seek his or her own profit before that of others; everyone would give him or herself to be taught by the Holy Spirit. By the mighty working of God's grace all were not only convinced but, as it were, carried along and mastered.

On 12 May 1748 Count Zinzendorf wrote:

Today, twenty-one years ago, the fate of Hernhutt hung in the balance, whether it was to become a sect, or to take its place in the Church. After an address of three or four hours, the power of the Holy Spirit decided for the latter. The foundation principle was laid down, that we were to set aside the thought of being Reformers, and to look after ourselves. What the Saviour did after that, up to the winter, cannot be expressed. The whole place was indeed a veritable dwelling of God with men; and on the 13th of August it passed into continual praise. It then quieted down, and entered the Sabbath rest.

12 May 1727 has been called the birthday of what was in future known as 'The Renewed Church'. Meanwhile, later that same year, on 13 August, a filling of the Holy Spirit was experienced. After the Statutes had been adopted and all had bound themselves to a life of obedience and love, the spirit of fellowship and prayer was greatly increased. Misunderstandings, prejudices and secret estrangements were confessed and put away, and prayer was often in such power that those who had only given external assent to the Statutes were convicted, and either changed or inwardly felt compelled to leave.

Count Zinzendorf had to leave home for a time, and on his return, 4 August, he brought with him a copy of the History of the Moravian Church that he had found, which gave the full account of the ancient discipline and order. This caused great joy among the people. It was taken as a token that the God of their fathers was with them. As one wrote:

> Under the cloud of our fathers we were baptised with their spirit; signs and wonders were seen among us, and there was great grace on the whole neighbourhood.

The whole of the next night was spent in prayer, with a great gathering in the hall at midnight. During the following days all were conscious in the singing meetings of a strange overwhelming power. On Sunday 10 August Pastor Rothe was leading the afternoon meeting at Hernhutt when he was overpowered and fell on his face before God. The whole congregation bowed under the sense of God's presence, and continued in prayer till midnight. He invited the congregation to the Holy Supper on the next Wednesday.

As it was the first communion since the new fellowship, it was resolved to be especially strict and to make use of it 'to lead the souls deeper into the death of Christ, into which they had been baptised'. The leaders visited every member, seeking in great love to lead that member to true heart searching. On the Tuesday evening, at the preparation service, several became believers as the whole community was deeply touched.

On that Wednesday morning all went to Berthelsdorf. On the way there, those who had felt estranged from another bound themselves together afresh. During the singing of the first hymn a wicked man was powerfully convicted. The presentation of the new communicants touched every heart, and while the hymn was being sung it could hardly be recognised whether there was more singing or weeping.

Several churches prayed:

- That they be kept free from separation and sectarianism.
- They asked the Lord to reveal to them the true nature of his church, so that they might walk before him, and might not abide alone but be made fruitful.
- They asked that they might do nothing contrary to the oath of loyalty they had taken to him, nor in the very least sin against his law of love.
- They asked that he would keep them in the saving power of his grace and not one of them be drawn away to self.
- They celebrated the Lord's Supper with hearts at the same time both bowed down and lifted up. Each went home greatly encouraged and spent the remainder of the day and the following days in great quiet and peace, and learning to love.

A number of children were among those present in the church when the communion was held. One member wrote:

> I cannot attribute the great revival among the children to anything else but that wonderful outpouring of the Holy Spirit on the communion assembly. The Spirit breathed in power on old and young. Everywhere they were heard, sometimes at night in the field, beseeching the Saviour to pardon their sins and make them his own. The Spirit of grace had indeed been poured out.

The church members frequently went out into the neighbourhood to have fellowship with other Christians and make Christ known to all who would come. When one of them was cast into prison for doing so, it caused great joy that that person was found worthy to suffer for his sake.

Their prayer watch

On 22 August 1727 it was recorded:

> Today, we considered how needful it is that our Church, which is as yet in her infancy and has in Satan such a mighty enemy, should guard herself against one who never slumbers day nor night, and have an unceasing holy watch kept against him. We resolved, therefore, to light a freewill offering of intercession which should burn night and day, leaving the matter for the present to God's working in the hearts of the Church.
>
> By the 26th the plan had ripened, and twenty-four brothers and twenty-four sisters each engaged to spend an hour, as fixed by lot, in their own rooms, to bring before God all the needs and interests of those around them. The number was soon increased. Since we wished to leave everything in Hernhutt to free grace and have nothing forced, we agreed that when anyone, from poverty of spirit or special business, could not spend the whole hour in prayer, he or she might instead praise God in spiritual songs, and so bring the sacrifice of praise or of prayer for him or herself and all saints.
>
> These watchers unto prayer met once a week. All news that had been received from far or near concerning the need of persons, congregations, or nations was passed on to them to lead to more hearty and definite prayer and to stir them to praise for answers given.

Their part in global mission

In the course of the following months some of the members were continually travelling, preaching and sharing the love of Christ. Zinzendorf kept in contact with all parts of the world and did not fail to communicate what he heard.

The following four years saw continual revival. The careful watch kept by the elders and superintendents; the faithful dealing with individual souls according to personal needs; the jealous maintenance of the spirit of loving unity; the continual prayer; the travelling into more distant regions made the assemblies of the church times of great joy and blessing. This was a time of preparation for the mission work that was to begin.

It came about in this way. In 1731 Count Zinzendorf had gone to Copenhagen to be present at the crowning of the King of Denmark. One of the nobles there had in his service a slave named Anton, who was from the West Indies. From him Zinzendorf heard of the condition of slaves in the West Indies, especially on the island of St Thomas, a Danish colony. He also met two Greenlanders, converts of the Danish missionary Hans Egede.

When he returned, the account he gave of meeting these people from unevangelised lands ignited deep interest in those present. Two members had their hearts particularly touched. Later that evening Zinzendorf said to a friend that he believed potential missionaries to the West Indies and Greenland would come forth from those present earlier in the meeting.

The slave, Anton, visited the community and gave an account concerning what slaves suffered and suggested that the Moravians also would suffer if they embarked upon witnessing in the West Indies. His testimony only made the fire burn more strongly. If it was difficult to approach the plantations to teach the slaves, the volunteers were ready to sell themselves as slaves to reach the poor lost souls.

It was not until a year later, in August 1732, that the first two missionaries left the Hernhutt community. The instructions were simply 'to see and be led of the Spirit in all things'.

They set off on foot, with nothing but a few coins in their purse, but with strong faith in God and his care. The next year two missionaries left for Greenland. In 1734 eighteen left for Santa Cruz, and in the following year twelve more, to attempt, by establishing settlements and industries, to help the slaves. And though this experiment cost many precious lives and was not a success, the church did not lose courage.

Lessons we can learn

Let us now turn to the main object for which the story of the Moravian Church has been told. It has been appealed to as an example. It was pointed out to us that, in proportion to its membership, the people it supports and sends out, the money it provides, the converts it has gathered, far exceed what any other church has done. In the first 20 years of its existence it actually sent out more missionaries than the whole Protestant Church had done in 200 years.

Let us ask how it happened that this little church, the least of all, has outdone all her older and larger sisters?

The answer appears to be this:

- She alone of all the churches has actually sought to carry out the great truth, that to gather in to Christ the souls he died to save is the one object for which the church exists.
- She alone has sought to teach and train all her members to count it their first duty to him who loved them to give their lives to make him known to others.

This answer at once leads to the further questions. What was it that led this church, at a time when she numbered only 300 members, to see and carry out these great truths? Which of her actions can we take and reproduce in our local churches?

It is only as we get some insight into this that we can find out what is needed if other churches are to profit by their example. There are three clear lessons we can learn and replicate. The first is addressed to leaders, the second to congregations, and the third involves prayer and the Holy Spirit.

Lessons for leaders

If we consider Zinzendorf, whom God had so wonderfully prepared to train and guide the young church in the path of global mission, we see at once what the great moving power was. What marked him above everything was a tender, childlike, passionate love of our Lord Jesus. Jesus Christ, the originator and inspirer of all mission work, possessed him. The dying love of the Lamb of God had won and filled his heart; the love which had brought Christ to die for sinners had come into his life; he could live for nothing else but sinners and die for them if need be. When he took charge of the Moravians, that love, as his teaching and his hymns testify, was the one motive to which he appealed, the one power he trusted, the one object for which he sought to win their lives. The love of Christ did what teaching and argument and discipline, however necessary and fruitful, never could have done. It melted all into one body; it made all willing to be corrected and instructed; it made all long to put away everything that was sin; it inspired all with the desire to testify of Jesus; it made many ready to sacrifice all in making that love known to others, and so making the heart of Jesus glad.

If the dying love of Christ were to take the place in our churches and their teaching, in our own hearts and fellowship with each other, which it had in theirs, which it has in God's heart and in Christ's redemption, would it not work a mighty change in our work and passion for global mission?

Along with this love of Christ, or rather, as the fruit of it, there was in Zinzendorf an intense sense of the need and the value of fellowship. He believed that love, to be enjoyed and to grow strong, and to attain its object, needs expression and communication. He believed that the love of Christ in us needs fellowship with each other for its maintenance in ourselves, as well as for the securing of God's great purpose in it – the comforting and strengthening of our each other. So he was prepared to take up the strangers God brought to him and give himself wholly to them. His reward was great. He was able to give himself to them and to find himself multiplied in each one. What he said later, 'I know of no true Christianity without fellowship,' was the principle that begat that intense unity which gave the strength of the leader and the whole body to each of its members.

In our Christianity there is a reticence in speaking of our personal relationship to Jesus, which often causes great loss. We forget that the majority of people are guided more by emotions than by intellect: the heart is the great power by which they are meant to be influenced and moulded. We might well take a lesson here from Zinzendorf.

A minister with his congregation, a teacher with her class, a leader in a prayer meeting or a youth group often works hard to influence by instruction and encouragement, while forgetting that hearts crave love, and that nothing can so help to build up the young or weak Christian life as the warm fellowship of love in Christ. There are thousands of Christians wishing to serve their Lord, but not knowing how, who are just longing to find gatherings where they can be helped to meet under a sense of the presence of our Lord Jesus and his love – where they can be helped to confess that love, and then to yield themselves to it in the faith that it will constrain and enable them to do anything their Lord needs them to do.

At the conference one speaker said:

> The importance of leadership must be emphasised. Let us put to work that talent which sets another to work. The leader must use definiteness and persistence. The leader must lift up biblical ideals.

And another:

> People become interested not so much in abstract ideas as in individuals who represent their ideas. Victories are won because people follow some leader whom they have learned to love.

Zinzendorf was indeed a mighty leader in whose footsteps we still may follow. Every church leader may learn from him the great secret – that the more intensely the fire of God's love burns in the heart, the more surely will it burn into those around us. It is the high privilege of leaders to know that God can give them such power over others, that their love for him can open their hearts for receiving more of the life and love and power of God. God's way is to dispense his blessings through individual men and women.

As each leader realises the privilege of being filled with fire for global mission and love and devotion of Christ Jesus, then living up to it through mission work at home will enter a new era. Life and love, passing from the living, loving Christ through a living, loving disciple, will communicate life and love to those who otherwise are cold and helpless.

Lessons for the congregation

What of the followers God had provided for the leader? Let the Moravian Church's history give the answer. There was first of all that detachment from the world and its hopes, that power of endurance, that simple trust in God, which suffering and persecution are meant to work. These people were literally strangers and pilgrims on earth. They were familiar with the thought and spirit of sacrifice. They had learnt to endure hardship and to look up to God in every trouble. It is this spirit which is still needed today. A disregard of what the world considers necessary or desirable; a self-denial that counts all but loss for the sake of knowing Christ and making him known; a trust in God that looks not only to his aid in special emergency, but for his guidance at every step and his power in every work.

The discipline the Moravians had inherited from their ancestors and to which they were led to yield to so completely at Hernhutt was rooted in the view that, to the Christian, faith is the all-important thing. Everything is secondary to the one great consideration – to know and do the will of God, to walk in the footsteps of Jesus Christ. For the sake of this they were ready to submit to the care and correction of all those appointed to watch over them. Believing literally in the command 'Exhort one another daily', they were willing to be reproved or warned as often as there was sin, either of omission or commission. When they were sent out, they were ready to help, to depend upon and to yield to each other. Their fellowship made them strong: all their leaders begged the people to tell what they might see wrong in them and there was a willingness to confess the slightest shortcoming. The spirit of subjection to one another, of which Scripture speaks so often, brought its rich blessing in sanctifying and strengthening the whole life.

To introduce the same discipline in our day may appear impossible. But the same spirit of watchful care of and loving subjection to one another is still within the reach of any circle that will seek for it, and will still be a wonderful preparation for effective work in God's Kingdom.

But there was still something more than this that gave the Moravian fellowship its wonderful power. It was the intensity of the Moravians' united and personal devotion to Jesus Christ, as the Lamb of God, who had purchased them with his blood. All their correction of each other and their willing confession and giving up of sin came from this faith in the living Christ, through whom they found 'within their hearts the peace of God and deliverance from the power of sin'. This faith led them to accept and jealously keep their place as poor sinners, saved by his grace, every day. This faith – cultivated and strengthened every day by fellowship in word and song and prayer – became the food of their life. This faith filled them with such joy that their hearts rejoiced, in the midst of the greatest difficulties, in the triumphant assurance that their Jesus, the Lamb who had died for them, and was now loving and saving and keeping them hour by hour, could conquer the hardest heart and was willing to bless the vilest sinner. In this spirit they met together for nearly five years, from the time of the first outpouring of the Spirit to the time the first missionaries went out. They continued worshipping the Son of God, offering themselves to him, and waiting for him to make known what he would have of his church, each one in readiness to go or do what the Lord should show.

Let a congregation, a prayer meeting, or any Christian group or mission agency seek to have this kind of spirit uniting the members, while all continue in prayer that the Lord would show each one his blessed will, and you have the beginning of a spirit that will spread. And as different congregations combine in making the worship and faith of the Lord Jesus and devotion to him the centre of their missionary interest, the number of those who are ready to go forth will speedily increase.

Prayer and the Holy Spirit

There is one thing more we must notice: the mighty moving of the Holy Spirit in answer to prayer. We have had Zinzendorf's testimony of how confident he was that the birth of the new church on 12 May 1727 was the work of the Spirit. We have read of the overwhelming sense of the Holy Spirit's presence in which she received her baptism from on high. Many a time after this during the following four years the records testify of special experiences of the deep movings of the Holy Spirit. This was mostly when they were gathered in prayer before their Lord. The prayer watch they appointed, so as to keep up day and night a continual sacrifice of supplication, proves what they understood heaven's first law to be that the measure of blessing and power will depend upon the measure of prayer. They saw and rejoiced exceedingly in the Lamb upon the throne – of course they could trust him to fill their mouths and hearts, so widely opened to him.

As at Pentecost, so at Hernhutt, united prayer, rewarded with the gift of the Spirit, was the entrance into the life of witness and victory, it is the law of all work in global mission. If the example of the Moravian Church is to stir us to jealousy, we must learn from them what it is to believe that we only exist to win the souls Jesus died to save. Then we must train our members to the thought that everyone must be ready for his service. We must learn the lesson of much prayer and of a definite surrender to have our whole lives under the leading of the Holy Spirit.

When we point to the example of the Moravians, the question is sometimes asked whether they have retained their first fire, whether their missionaries and members are still living on a higher spiritual level than the churches around them.

The answer is very simple: like every other church, the Moravians have had their times of decline and revival. They were too closely one with the church around them not to suffer with it when the cold of winter came. The force of our appeal is not weakened, however, but strengthened by this fact. Its point is this. The three great principles taught by the Holy Spirit in any time of his mighty working are these:

- That the church exists only for extending the Kingdom of God.
- That every member must be trained to take part in it.
- That the personal experience of the love of Christ is the power that fits for this.

To these principles the Moravians have remained true, and it is in this respect that their example speaks to us with such power.

The church of Christ owes more to the Moravian Church than is generally known. From her, John Wesley received that joyful assurance of acceptance which gave his preaching such power, and fitted him as God's instrument not only to found the Wesleyan Church, but to take such an important part in the revival of evangelical faith in England. William Carey owed part of his inspiration for global mission to them. When pleading with his fellow Baptists, he backed his proposals by the experience of the Moravians, and laid upon the table the Periodical Accounts of the Moravian Church. His companion, William Ward, recorded the profound impression produced on his mind by these Periodic Accounts, and exclaimed, 'Thank you, Moravians! You have done me good! If I am ever a missionary worth a straw, I shall, under our Saviour, owe it to you.'

The story of the wondrous grace of God in the Moravians may still show us the path and inspire the courage to seek and find new blessing for the world.

8

Going Still Deeper

Introduction

Richard Foster writes in his book *Celebration of Discipline*:

> Superficiality is the curse of our age. The doctrine of instant satisfaction is a primary spiritual problem. The desperate need today is not for a greater number of intelligent people, or gifted people, but for deep people.[1]

Writers and leaders through the ages have commented on the superficial nature and decline in peoples' spiritual lives. Perhaps today, though, such superficiality and desire for instant spiritual satisfaction is compounded by the individualism that characterises our culture and worldview.

Shortly after the deaths of Princess Diana and Mother Teresa commentators were comparing the two women and commending them for what they had achieved in their lives, saying that both had had a positive impact on the world. However, the differences between the two women are significant, and the comparison is at the heart of the Christian faith. Diana was a princess who lived in a palace and occasionally left that palace to visit the poor and marginalised. Mother Teresa, on the other hand, lived

[1] Richard Foster, *Celebration of Discipline* (Hodder & Stoughton, 1980), p. 1.

among the poor and marginalised and occasionally visited a princess in a palace.

I see within myself and within many a desire to follow the princess model of living: to live in comfortable surroundings with our daily needs met and occasionally to venture out on our own terms to show our benevolence to the marginalised. However, we fail to recognise that we are not all called to be royal princesses – we fail by not having such a family lineage, the opportunities or background. However, any one of us could be a Mother Teresa, as what she did was take seriously the command of Jesus to consider and treat the poor as he would and be willing to pay the price for doing so.

This chapter is an uncomfortable one to read and is not for the faint-hearted! Andrew Murray sets out the conditions and directions, focused on personal spiritual discipline, for going deeper in commitment to Christ.

In Chapter 1 we looked at how, when developing a Mission Lifestyle, there is a need for faith to work. Here Murray takes this still further and suggests that faith will only work when it is put into action. By using the story and experiences of Hudson Taylor he maintains that faith needs training.

As you read and follow Andrew Murray's exercise plan for deepening faith and commitment to Christ, begin to assess and think how you can develop these same principles to put them into practice.

* * * * *

Going Still Deeper

Paul wrote to the Corinthians that because there was strife and division among them they were still worldly and not spiritual.

I could not address you as spiritual but as worldly – mere infants in Christ. I gave you milk, not solid food, for you were not yet ready for it. Indeed, you are still not ready. You are still worldly. For since there is jealousy and quarrelling among you, are you not worldly? Are you not acting like mere men? (1 Cor. 3:1–3).

One chief mark of the desire to be truly spiritual is the desire not to sin, to be delivered from the common sins of which the average Christian is so tolerant. When this desire ripens into faith, the person is brought into an altogether fresher and clearer consciousness of Christ's power to save, and learns how broad and deep is the meaning of faith. The believer then lives by the faith of him who loved us and gave of himself, and now lives in us, and is himself our keeper.

What has this to do with global mission? Such a new experience of what Christ has done leads to a larger trust in what he can do for others. This gives both reason and courage in testifying of him. It brings a new tone into a person's preaching or speaking. Christ becomes more distinctly the centre of all thought and all work; at the same time the source, subject and strength of all our witness. Along with this the claims of Christ, his call for our devotion, loyalty and total surrender, become clearer. It is seen that absolute consecration, which at conversion was hardly understood, is both our duty and our highest privilege. And work for Christ, or rather a life wholly given up to live for him and for the people he loves, becomes the unceasing aim of the liberated soul.

In the teaching of these truths emphasis is placed on the mighty saving power of Christ, on the sin of limiting him, on the call to honour him by an unbounded trust, and on his claims to a life wholly devoted to his will and service. The transition from the thought of faith and consecration as related to personal blessing, to their application in a life given up to winning people to the Saviour, is simple and sure. Many have found that what at first was sought for the sake of personal blessing becomes the power for living to be a blessing to others. So the deepening of the Christian life becomes the power of a new devotion to global mission and the Kingdom of our Lord. This is the lesson the whole church of Christ may learn from it in her search for the key to the challenge of global mission.

It may appear difficult or impossible to move our whole denominations or agencies simultaneously, so as to get the life really deepened and fitted for the tremendous work that has been undertaken in this generation. Let the beginning be made in single local congregations. Let the church leadership learn and teach that all failure in caring, giving, praying and desire for global mission is owing to a weak and inadequate superficial spiritual life. Let leaders call upon their people to follow them as they seek to lead them to a deeper spiritual life. Let them speak of sin, and Christ as Saviour from it; of faith in Christ as able to do more than we have experienced or expected; of entire consecration, the giving up of our will and all we have, to be wholly under the control of our Lord, as the only door to abiding happiness and true service.

Let the leaders plead with their people, by the love and honour of Christ, by the need of the unreached, by the inconceivable privilege of being made the channel of the divine life to the souls of men and women, to come and be wholehearted for Christ. Let them speak of work for Christ among those near or far as the one thing by which we can prove our faith and love. Let them gather the people to pray for the Holy Spirit's working in them to equip them for mission work. Let them encourage the faith that, if hearts give themselves in simplicity to their Lord, expecting his guidance, he will show what he would have them do.

As both the deepening of the spirit life and devotion to global mission are sought after, the one will react on the other, because both have their root in Jesus Christ himself, revealed afresh as Saviour and Lord.

When such a rediscovery of Christ takes place, a new relationship is established. Prayer becomes the spontaneous turning of the believer, or of a company of believers, to him who has proved his power to them. They know that the power will come from him for all they have to do, and on all the work that is done.

For the sad complaint of lack of time or heart for prayer, for the vain call to more prayer, there is but one cure – the deepening of the spiritual life. The challenge of global mission is a personal one. Lead people to the deliverance there is in Christ. Lead them from the half-hearted, worldly life in which they have lived back to the 'first love' of a personal attachment and devotion to the living, loving Christ. Then they will see that there is no life worth living but that of devotion to his Kingdom.

Prayer, private and public, will flow, and the blessing it draws down from heaven will prepare the church to labour as it has never yet done, and to see blessing above all we can ask or think.

The challenge of global mission is a personal one. Seek of the spiritual life, then consecration and global mission will follow.

The power of believing prayer

At the New York Ecumenical Missionary Conference the China Inland Mission[2] was frequently mentioned. Under the leadership of one man of faith, Hudson Taylor, God had, over a 30-year period, led out 600 missionaries. All had gone without any guarantee of funds for their support beyond what God might give in answer to believing prayer.

If the church at large is to profit by this example, it is well that all Christians who take part in the support of missions should know what was the secret of its power. It is not necessary to copy its methods and organisation. But there is urgent need everywhere throughout the church for learning how the power of God can be brought into global mission work.

Training and practice

At the conference Hudson Taylor spoke of the source of power for Christian mission and gave an example of what the power of believing prayer is. I quote from his speech:

> It is not lost time to wait upon God. In November 1886, we in the China Inland Mission were feeling greatly the need of Divine guidance in the matters of organisation and reinforcements of labourers. We came together to spend eight days in united waiting upon God, four alternate days being days of fasting as well as prayer. We were led to pray for a hundred labourers to be sent out by our English Board during 1887. In this connection we needed to ask God for $50,000, in addition to the income of the previous year. We were guided to pray that this might be given in large sums, so that our staff might not be unduly occupied in the acknowledgement of contributions.
>
> What was the result? God sent us offers of service from over six hundred men and women during the following year, and those considered ready and suitable were accepted and sent out to China. At the end of the year exactly one hundred had gone! Further, God did not give us exactly the $50,000 we asked for, but He gave us $55,000 which came in eleven

---

[2] Now known as the Overseas Missionary Fellowship (OMF).

contributions: the smallest was $2500, the largest was $12,500. We had a thanksgiving for the new workers and the money.

The power of the living God is available power. We may call upon Him in the name of Christ, with the assurance that if we are taught by the Spirit in our prayers, those prayers will be answered.

Where and how had the secret of such believing prayer been learnt? Was it a gift bestowed by divine favour on a chosen one, which others cannot expect to receive? Or was it the result of training and practising, the reward of faithfulness in little things, to teach us that we, too, can walk in the same path? It was indeed a gift, as every grace is a gift of God bestowed in different measure as he pleases. But it was at the same time the outcome of a life of trial and obedience, by which the gift that had been only a little, hidden, unconscious seed had been developed. It had grown strong so that all God's children might be encouraged to walk in his footsteps, with the assurance that to each one the path of prevailing prayer stands open.

Listen to the story of how Hudson Taylor learnt about the power of believing prayer:

> Not many months after my conversion, having a leisure afternoon, I went to my room to spend it largely in communion with God. Well do I remember that occasion. In the gladness of my heart, I poured out my heart before God. Again and again, I confessed my grateful love to Him who had done everything for me. God had saved me when I had given up all hope and even wish for salvation. I asked Him to give me some work to do for Him as an outlet for my love and gratitude: some self-denying service, no matter what it might be, however trying or however trivial. I asked for something with which He would be pleased and that I might do directly for Him who had done so much for me.

Well do I remember, as in unreserved consecration I put myself, my life, my friends, my all upon the altar, the deep solemnity that came over my soul with the assurance that my offering was accepted. The presence of God became unutterably real and blessed. Though I was only a boy of fifteen, I remember stretching myself on the ground, and lying there silent before Him with unspeakable awe and unspeakable joy. For what service I was accepted I did not know; but a deep consciousness that I was no longer my own took possession of me, which has never since left me. Within a few months of this time of consecration the impression came into my soul that the Lord wanted me in China.

Consecration is always the outcome of a powerful conversion and the secret of a life in which power in prayer and faith is to be acquired. Some are inclined to look upon it as an attainment and an end when its true value consists in it being a beginning, a putting oneself into God's hands to prepare for his service. It is only the entrance into the higher class of the school where God himself teaches how he desires us to serve.

Hudson Taylor still had much to learn before he could become the man of faith who could be a witness to what God can do. In thinking of going to China he felt that he wanted to do so in faith, trusting God for the supply of his needs. If he was to trust him in China, why not learn to trust him in England? Failure in China might be fatal: he would ask God to teach him at home how to walk in faith. He understood the command 'owe no man anything' to be meant literally: however great his need might be, he would speak to none but God about it.

Exercising faith

One story out of his many experiences at this time illustrates how his faith was trained:

My employer wished me to remind him when my salary became due. I determined to ask God to remind him of it, and so encourage me by answering prayer. At the end of a certain quarter, when my salary was due, one Saturday night I found that I had only a single coin. Still I had no lack, and I continued in prayer.

That Sunday after the church service in the morning, the rest of the day was filled with gospel work as usual in the lowest part of the town. After my last service at ten o'clock that night, a poor man asked me to go and pray with his wife, as she was dying, and the priest had refused to come without payment. The man could not produce this because the family was starving. It flashed into my mind at once that all the money I possessed was the solitary coin. Moreover, though I had porridge sufficient for supper and for breakfast, I had nothing for dinner the next day.

At once there was a stoppage of the flow of joy in my heart. Instead of correcting myself, I began to criticise the poor man.

'Ah,' thought I, 'if only I two coins, how gladly would I give these poor people one of them!' The truth of the matter was that I could trust God plus one coin, but could not trust Him only, without any money.

The poor man led me into a court where, on my last visit, I had been roughly handled. I followed up a miserable flight of stairs, and into a room where four or five starved-looking children stood about, and on a pallet lay the mother, with a tiny babe, thirty-six hours old, moaning at her side.

'Ah,' thought I, 'if only I two coins, how gladly would I give these poor people one of them!' Still unbelief prevented me from relieving their distress at the cost of all I possessed.

Strange to say, I could not comfort these people. I told them not to be cast down, for they had a kind, loving Father in heaven; but something said to me, 'You hypocrite, speaking about a kind, loving Father when you are not prepared to trust Him without money!' I nearly choked. If I had only had one more coin! – but I was not yet ready to trust God with nothing.

In those days prayer was usually a delight to me; so I tried to pray, but when I opened my lips with 'Our Father which art in heaven,' prayer seemed a mockery, and I passed through such a time of conflict as I have never experienced before or since. I arose from my knees in great distress.

The father turned to me and said, 'Sir, if you can help us, for God's sake do!' and the word flashed into my mind, 'Give to him that asks.' Slowly, taking the single coin from my pocket, I gave it to the him, saying that I was giving him my all, but that God was really a Father and might be trusted. All the joy came back to my heart, and the hindrance to blessing was gone – gone, I trust, forever.

Not only was the woman's life saved, but I was saved too. My Christian life might have been a wreck had the striving of God's Spirit not been obeyed. I went home, my heart as light as my pocket. As I knelt at my bedside, I reminded the Lord that 'he who giveth to the poor lendeth to the Lord'; and with peace within and peace without, I spent a restful night.

Next morning, at breakfast, I was surprised to see my landlady come in with a letter in her hand. I could not recognise the handwriting or the postmark, and where it came. On opening the envelope I found, inside a sheet of blank paper, a pair of kid gloves, and as I opened them, four coins fell to the ground. 'Praise the Lord!' I exclaimed; 'four hundred percent for twelve hours' investment!

This incident proves what training is needed in private before we are allowed in public to become witness to the power of faith in God and that it is prevailing prayer which brings it about. They teach us that, if our mission is to be a work in which the power of believing prayer is to be displayed, the faith of individual believers must have its roots deeply fixed in true consecration to God, and in

powers are. The power of separation from the world and true self-sacrifice, of intense attachment and devotion to Jesus, of love and fellowship making us one with the saints around us, of faith and of continued prayer. These things made the disciples ready to receive the promise of the Father and be the fit instruments for the Holy Spirit's mighty work in witnessing for Christ to the end parts of the earth.

People are wonderfully formed to have, in human nature, as Jesus had, the Spirit of God dwelling in them. How wonderful this blessing was in itself – the fruit and the crown of Christ's redeeming work. These people, prepared by Christ, were all filled with the Holy Spirit.

On earth Christ's Body had been the home of the Spirit and the instrument of his work. Mortal people are now his Body; they take his place; the Spirit dwells in them as the instruments for the continuance of Christ's own work. The Spirit, through whom God is God, and Father and Son, each is what he is, and both are One – that Spirit, the very life of God, fills them.

In the threefold operation of his grace, he enlightens, he sanctifies, he strengthens. That is, he reveals divine truth, he makes us partakers of the holy life and disposition of Christ, and he endues us with the divine power that, in the midst of weakness, triumphs through us.

'But you will receive power when the Holy Spirit comes on you ... ' (Acts 1:8). God's power for God's work was to be the one condition of success in their undertaking to bring the gospel to the ends of the earth. That Pentecost generation did more to accomplish this than any succeeding generation. Considering the increase in the population of the world and the increase of the church, we ought to do tenfold more than they did. But even if we are to do as much as they did, we need this one thing: to be filled with the Holy Spirit, as the power of God, to do the work of God!

It is not enough that the river of the water of life is still flowing from under the throne of God and the Lamb; it is not enough that we are the temple of God, and the Spirit of God dwells in us. The Spirit may be in us, and yet be grieved, or quenched, or resisted, or neglected. Where he is in power, he asks to fill the whole being. He claims control of the whole life. We are to be led and ruled by him in everything. He asks that humanity shall be a living sacrifice, a whole burnt offering, to be consumed by the fire of God.

If there is to be any hope of our working like the early church, we must have a new era in global missions. There must be a real restoration of the Pentecost life and power in the local church. The power of God for the work of God must be the watchword of every worker. Only then will our participation in global mission, both in its extent and its intensity, be able to reach those who are still without the knowledge of Christ.

If we are to take this seriously, what are we to do about it? We must confess that the overwhelming majority of our church members are very far from Pentecost. What is to be done to get all our leaders in churches and agencies to take up the watchword: back to Pentecost? Without this the work cannot be done.

We must gather our church leaders, congregations and all who feel that God's work is not being done as it should be into one holy bond of union until the watchword has echoed through the church: back to Pentecost; God's power for God's work. Without this the work cannot be done.

The challenge of global mission is a personal one. Every believer, in receiving the love of Christ into his or her heart, has taken in a love that reaches out to the whole world. The Great Commission rests on every member of the church. Let each of us begin to seek for the church the restoration of her Pentecost power for the work of conquering the world for her King.

It was intense, continued, united prayer that brought Pentecost. That prayer did not cease until it was answered. Such prayer is not an easy thing.

Hudson Taylor said:

> Not only must mission workers suffer in going forth, but the Church must go forward in self-denial to the point of suffering. Redemptive work, soul-saving work, cannot be carried on without suffering. If we are simply to pray as a pleasant and enjoyable exercise, and know nothing of watching in prayer, and weariness in prayer, we shall not draw down the available blessing. We shall not sustain our mission workers, who are overwhelmed with the appalling darkness of the world; we shall not even sufficiently maintain the spiritual life of our own souls. We must serve God even to the point of suffering; each one must ask themself, 'To what degree, at what point, am I extending, by personal suffering, by personal self-denial even to the point of pain, the kingdom of Christ?

Let us give ourselves again to prayer, that the church may be restored to her Pentecost state. Let us by faith yield ourselves wholly to the Spirit and receive the Spirit by faith to fill us. Let us give ourselves to prayer for the power of the Spirit in the life and work of the church local and global. The Pentecost command to preach the gospel to every creature is urgent, all the more from having been neglected so long. Prayer brought Pentecost. Prayer still brings it. But few feel how weak our power in prayer is.

What was it that started those people praying like that? It was this one thing: Jesus Christ had their whole heart. They had given up and placed down everything for him. His love filled them and made them one with him and with each other. The fellowship of love strengthened them. Their ascended Lord was everything to them; they couldn't help praying. Let us pray in secret. Let us unite in love with others and pray without ceasing, and watch unto prayer that, for the sake of his Son and a perishing world, God will restore his people to their first estate in the devotion and power and joy of Pentecost. Let us always remember: the challenge of global mission is personal one. A passionate love to Jesus Christ, born out of his love for us, truly possessing each of us personally, will teach us to pray, to labour and to suffer. Let us pray for such a love.

10

The Challenge Of Global Mission Is Personal

Introduction

One of the classic modern-day Christian authors who follows in the tradition of Andrew Murray, C.S. Lewis or A.W. Tozer is Philip Yancey. His book *What's so Amazing about Grace?* [1] has encouraged many to refocus on grace.

When I first got hold of this book in 1997 it helped me to re-evaluate my faith and ministry. It is so easy to acknowledge and then forget because of great familiarity the grace that Christ has proven and lavished up on us. Like following a familiar country path, one can lose sight of the beauty of creation. Or in a loving marriage the close acquaintance can lead to not verbalising the love and devotion to each other. One reason for why this occurs is silent conscious and subconscious assumptions. 'I don't need to tell my wife I love her, because she knows,' commented a friend to me. Meanwhile, his wife was confiding to Denice, my wife, that she wished he would say 'I love you'.

---

[1] Philip Yancey, *What's so Amazing about Grace?* (Zondervan, 1997).

When we become too familiar or assume too much from God's grace without consciously acknowledging the cost, pain and sacrifice involved, this is grace abuse. And when grace abuse begins to occur we gradually fail to live or follow in the light of the love of Christ. Our faith might be sincere, but sincerely empty of grace.

Back in 1997, when I read about God's grace in Yancey's book, I was awestruck and gradually began to realise that stepping out and developing a Mission Lifestyle was not solely dependant on the command to go into all the world. It is equally founded upon the motivation of God's grace, which catapulted me into realising afresh the need for compassion for the world. As Yancey shares, 'There is nothing we can do to make God love us more. There is nothing we can do to make God love us less.'[2] Surely this is reason enough, when placed alongside the commands of Christ, to go, share and demonstrate in every way possible this grace we have received?

Throughout Andrew Murray's writing, and particularly in the chapter that follows, such grace plays an essential part, one that he saw could be played by every believer. Hence his phrase 'Every believer a living witness' to describe how all members of the community of believers have an essential role and part to play in global mission. It is not just for the fanatical few of us!

* * * * *

The Challenge of Global Mission is a Personal One

Christ meant every believer to be a living witness. Or rather, every believer has been saved by grace with the express purpose that he or she should make known this

---

[2] Ibid., p. 70.

saving grace to others. This should be the supreme end of a believer's existence in the world.

If ever I feel the need of the teaching of the Holy Spirit for myself and my readers it is when I come to this point. We so easily accept general statements without realising fully what they imply. It is only when we are brought face to face with them, and challenged to apply and act upon them, that the secret unbelief comes out that robs them of their power. Only by the Holy Spirit can we look beyond the present state of the church and the great majority of Christians and realise what actually is the will of our God concerning his people and what he has actually made possible to them in the grace of his Holy Spirit.

As local church leaders, when we teach the church our motto must be 'Every believer a living witness!' This alone will give a sure foundation for our appeal for global mission, and our hope for an immediate and a sufficient response to the call to make Christ known to every person.

But is the statement 'Every believer a living witness' literally true and binding? Is it not something impractical? Is it not something beyond the reach of the majority of believers?

The very fact that this truth seems strange to so many and so difficult for any but the spiritually minded to grasp as possible and obligatory is the most urgent reason to teach it. Let us see the grounds on which it rests.

Nature teaches us that it must be so: it is an essential part of the new nature. We see it in every child who loves to tell of his or her excitement at what he or she has been given or achieved. We expect to find in every human heart a feeling of compassion for the poor and the suffering. So why should it be thought strange that every child of God is called to take part in making known the happiness he or she has found, to concern him or herself about those who do not know grace, to have compassion on them and work for their salvation? 'Every believer a living witness!' What can be more natural?

Christ called his disciples 'the light of the world'. The believer is an intelligent being; his or her light does not shine as a blind force of nature, but is the voluntary reaching out of his or her heart towards those who are in darkness. The believer longs to bring the light to them, to do all he or she can to acquaint them with Christ Jesus. The light is often used to illustrate the silent influence that good works and a consistent life may have. Yes, this is an essential element, but it means a great deal more. It does not mean, as is often thought, that I am to be content with finding my own salvation, and trusting that my example will do others good. No! Even as Christ's example derived its power from the fact that it was a life lived for us and given up on our behalf, so the true power of the Christian's influence lies in the love that gives itself away in seeking the happiness of others. As God is light and love, it is love that makes the Christian the light of the world. 'Every Believer a living witness' – this is indeed the law of the Spirit of life in Christ Jesus.

How could it be otherwise? As God is love, so are we that love born of God. Love is God's highest glory, his everlasting blessedness. God's children bear his image, share his blessedness and are the heirs of his glory. But this cannot be in any other way than by their living a life of love. The new life in them is a life of love: how can it manifest itself but in loving as God loves, in loving those whom God loves?

It is God's own love that is shed abroad in our hearts. Christ prayed:

> I have made you known ... and will continue to make you known in order that the love you have for me may be in them and that I myself may be in them (Jn. 17:26).

It is the love of Christ, the love with which he loves us, that constrains us. Love cannot change its nature when it flows down from God into us: it still loves the evil ones and the unworthy. Now that Christ is in heaven, the most basic way for his love to reach all of humanity in this age – for whom he died and for whom he longs – is through us. Surely nothing can be more natural and true than the blessed message 'Every believer redeemed to be a living witness.'

Two secrets revealed

But why, if it is so simple, are so many words needed to prove and enforce this? Because the church is in a weak and sickly state, and tens of thousands of her members have never learnt that this is one of the choicest treasures of their heritage. They are content with the selfish thought of personal salvation and blessing, and even in the struggle for holiness never learn the real purpose for their salvation. And there are tens of thousands more who have some thought of its being part of their calling, yet who have looked upon it as a command beyond their strength. They have never known that, as a law and a power of their innermost nature, its fulfilment is meant to be a normal function of a healthy body in joy and strength.

Even the commandments of Jesus may be to us as great a burden as the Law of Moses, bringing bondage and condemnation, unless we know the twofold secret that brings the power of performance. That secret is firstly what we have already named: the faith that love is the inward law of our new nature, and that the Spirit of God's law is within us to enable us gladly to love, bless and save those around us.

Secondly, it is in the surrender to a life of following and continual fellowship with the Lord Jesus – rejoicing in him, committing all to him, yielding all to the service of his love and grace – that our spiritual nature can be strengthened. Then the work of winning others becomes the highest joy and fulfilment of the Christian life. To those who in some measure understand this, there is nothing strange in the thought: 'Every believer a living witness!'

This ought to be the theme of every church leader's preaching and every believer's life.

But even this is not all. Many will agree that every believer is called upon to live and work for others, but still looks upon this as only a secondary thing, additional and subordinate to the primary interest of working out his or her own salvation. 'Every believer a living witness': this does not mean among other things, but first of all, as the chief reason of existence.

He chose us

We all agree in saying that the one and supreme end of the church is to bring the world to Christ. We know that God gave him the church as his Body. The one purpose was that the church should be to her head what every body is on earth – the living organ or instrument through which the purposes and the work of the head can be carried out. What is true of the head is true of the Body; what is true of the Body is true of each individual member – even the very weakest. As in the head, Christ Jesus, as in the Body, the church, so in every believer, the supreme, the sole end of our being is the saving of souls. It is in this, above everything, that God is glorified. 'I chose you and appointed you to go and bear fruit – fruit that will last' (Jn. 15:16).

Many may be brought to agree to this truth and yet have to confess that they do not feel its full force. Many local church leaders may feel how little they are able to preach it, compared with the full conviction with which they preach grace for salvation. It is well that we should give such confessions careful consideration. Where does the difficulty come in? This union with the Lord Jesus, to participate in his saving work to such an extent that without us he cannot do it, that through us he will and can accomplish it in divine power, is a deep spiritual mystery. It is an honour altogether too great for us to understand. It is a fellowship and union and partnership so intimate and divine that the Holy Spirit alone must reveal it to us.

Losing our first love

Some have lived long in the Christian life and lost their first love, and to them everything has to come by the slow way of the understanding. Such people need humility to give up preconceived opinions and the confidence of being able to grasp spiritual truths. They also need patient waiting for the Spirit to work such truth in their inmost parts. Above all, we need to turn away from the world, with its spirit and wisdom, and return to closer fellowship with Jesus Christ, as from him alone come light and love. Every believer is to be first and foremost a living witness. Simple though it sounds, it will cost much to many before they have mastered this.

We are often at a loss to understand the need for much continued communion with God. And yet it is the same as with the things of the earth. Take the gold put into the furnace. Exposed to insufficient heat, it gets heated, but not melted. Exposed to an intense heat for only a short time, and then taken out again, it is not melted. It needs an intense and continuous heat before the precious but hard metal is prepared for the goldsmith's work. So it is with the fire of God's love. Those who would know it in its power, and in power proclaim and convey it to others, must keep in contact with the love of Christ. They must know it in its intensity, and know what it is to continue in it till their whole being realises that that love can reach all and melt all. It can make even the coldest and weakest child of God a lover and living witness. In that intense and continuous fire a church leader can learn to witness in power to the truth: 'Every believer a living witness'.

Living witnesses as part of the Body

Let us consider again the illustration of the head and the body. The lessons are so obvious. The head can do nothing but through the body. Each member is as completely under the control of the head as the whole body. If the members, owing to disease, refuse to act, the head is help-less to carry out its plans. The object of the head is, firstly, to use every member for the preservation and welfare of the whole body, and then to let it take its share in the work the body has to do. If our being members of Christ's Body has any meaning, every believer is in the Body to care for the other members, and all to co-operate with the others in working out the plans of the head. Wherever I go, what-ever I do, I carry every member of my body with me, and they take part in all I do.

It is the same in the Body of Christ Jesus. Every member has only one objective and, while healthy, is every moment fulfilling that objective: to carry out the work of the head. The work of our Head in heaven is to gather all the members of his Body on earth. In this work every member of the Body co-operates, not under the law of a blind force of nature, but under the law of the Spirit of life, which connects every believer with her Lord in love, and imparts to her the same disposition and the same strength in which Christ does his work. Each time we read of Christ the head and his Body the church, let us with new emphasis pronounce the motto: 'Every member, like Christ, a living witness'.

What has this to do with our discussion of global mission? We seek to make it the keynote of this book: the challenge of global mission is a personal one. If the church is really to take up its work, it is not enough that we speak of the obligation resting upon the present generation to make Christ known to everyone. True education must always deal with the individual mind. To the general command must always be added the personal one. Admiral Lord Nelson's signal to his crew at the battle of Trafalgar – 'England expects every man to do his duty' – was a personal appeal addressed to every seaman, not just his fleet.

As we seek to find out why, when there are millions of Christians, the real army of God that is fighting the hosts of darkness is so small, the only answer is lack of heart. The enthusiasm for the Kingdom is missing. And that is because there is so little enthusiasm for the King of Kings. Though much may be done by careful organisation and strict discipline and good leadership to make the best of the few workers we have, there is nothing that can so restore confidence and courage as the actual presence of a beloved King, to whom every heart beats warm in loyalty and devotion.

The appeal for participation in global mission must go deeper and seek to deal with this very root. If there is no desire to be a living witness at home, how can the interest in global mission be truly deep or spiritual? There may be many motives to which we appeal effectively in asking for supplies of workers and money – the compassion of a common humanity or the elevation of fellow human beings in the scale of human life. But the true and highest motive is the only one that will really call forth the spiritual power of the church, for the work to be done.

If the appeal for global mission to this generation is to be successful, the church will have to gird itself for the work in a very different way from what it has been doing. The most serious question the church has to face just now (in fact, the only real difficulty of the challenge of global mission) is how she is to be awakened as a whole to the greatness and glory of the task entrusted to her and led to engage in it with all her heart and strength. The only answer to that question and the key to the whole situation appears to me to be the simple truth: the challenge of global mission is a personal one.

The Lord Jesus Christ is the Author and Leader of global mission. Whoever stands right with him and abides in him will be ready to know and do his will. It is simply a matter of being near enough to him to hear his voice, and so devoted to him and his love as to be ready to do all his will. Christ's relationship with each of us is an intensely personal one. He loved me and gave himself for me. My relationship with him is an entirely personal one. He gave himself as a ransom for me, and I am his, to live for him and his glory. He has breathed his love into my heart, and I love him. He tells me that, as a member of his Body, he needs me for his service, and in love I gladly yield myself to him. He wants nothing more than that I should tell this to others, prove to them how he loves, how he enables us to love, and how blessed is a life in his love.

The personal element of the challenge of global mission must be put in the foreground. Every global mission sermon or meeting must give the love of Christ the first place. If Christians are in a low, cold, worldly state, the first object must be to wait on God in prayer and faith for his Holy Spirit to lead them to a true devotion to Jesus Christ. Will that be an apparent loss of time in not beginning at once with the ordinary mission worker information and pleas? Ah, no – it will soon be made up. Weak believers, who are glad to hear and give, must be lifted to the consciousness of the wonderful spiritual privilege of offering themselves to Christ to live for his Kingdom. They must be encouraged to believe that the Lord, who loves them, greatly prizes their love, and will enable them to bring it to him. They must learn that Christ's dying love asks for wholehearted devotion, and that the more they sacrifice the more that love will possess them. As definitely as we labour to secure the interest and the gifts of each individual, even more so must we labour to bring each one into contact with Christ himself.

At first it may appear as if we are aiming too high. In many congregations the response may be very weak. Let the church leader give him or herself to study the challenge of global mission in this light. Let he or she put it to the congregation, clearly and perseveringly: You have been redeemed to be the witnesses and messengers of Christ's love. To fit you for it, his love has been given you, and shed abroad in your heart. As he loves you, he loves the whole world. He wants those who know it to tell those who don't know it. His love to you and to them, your love to him and to them, calls you to do it. It is your highest privilege; it will be your highest happiness and perfection. As Christ gave himself, give yourself wholly to this work of love.

11

The Responsibility of Leaders in Global Mission

Introduction

When Jesus was alone in the garden in John 17 his prayer was bound up with himself and his ministry, his relationship and preparation of the disciples for their future ministry, and the future ministry of 'those who will believe in me through their message' (verse 20). This really is an example of a leader at prayer for those he leads.

Knowing what he was about to meet in his arrest, trial and death, it seems quite justified that Jesus should only pray for himself. We probably would not see this as selfish but rather as preparation for what was to come. As a leader under pressure, it is easier to pray for yourself than for those you lead and definitely easier than for those you cannot see or hear. Yet Christ prayed for his disciples and future disciples as well as for himself because he knew that the three were inextricably linked. These three are interconnected and each is linked to the other because all were focused on one goal: the purposes of God the Father, Son and Spirit.

Through studying and using this prayer as a framework for my own prayer life, I have discovered and believe that this element of Christian leadership is often forgotten or overlooked. Christ prayed for himself so that he would lead well and with integrity, honour and truth; he prayed for his disciples so that they would be protected and grow in strength, love and unity; and he prayed for the extension of the church because he knew that what he was building would last for generations. It was eternal.

In this chapter Andrew Murray once again speaks to leaders and suggests that we should not only become imitators of Christ, but also suggests practical ways in which this can be achieved. Then we too can pray like Christ did in John 17.

* * * * *

The Responsibility of Leaders in Global Mission

In the chapter 'Responses to the Ecumenical Missionary Conference' a number of quotations were given in which the responsibility for the solution to the challenge of global mission was, with common consent, laid upon the Christian leadership. To the pastor belongs the privilege and responsibility for the challenge of global mission. That a holy and heavy responsibility rests on the ministry in this matter all will surely agree.

However, let all church leaders heartily admit and accept it and prepare themselves to live up to it. What is the ground on which that responsibility rests? The principles out of which it grows are simple, and yet of inconceivable importance.

They are these:

- That global mission is the chief end of the church.
- That the chief end of the ministry is to guide the church in this work and equip her for it.

- That the chief end of the preaching to a congregation ought to be to train it to help to fulfil her destiny.
- That the chief end of every church leader in this connection ought to be to fit him or herself thoroughly for this work.

These statements are not exaggerated. They may appear to be because we have been so accustomed to give global mission a very subordinate place in our church and ministry. We need to be brought back to the great central truth and mystery of God, that the church is the Body of Christ, absolutely and exclusively ordained by God to carry out the purpose of his redeeming grace-filled love in the world.

The church has only one objective: to be the light of the world. As Christ died for everyone, as God wills that all people should be saved, so the Spirit of God in the church knows only this purpose: the gospel should be brought to every creature. Global mission is the chief end of the church. All the work of the Holy Spirit in converting sinners and edifying believers has this for its one aim: to fit global mission for the part that each must take in winning back the world to God. Nothing other than God's eternal purpose can be the goal of the church.

As we see this to be true, we shall see that the chief end of the ministry ought to be to equip the church for this. Paul writes,

> It was he who gave ... some to be pastors and teachers, to prepare God's people for works of service, so that the body of Christ may be built up' (Eph. 4:11–12).

Paul gives us insight as to what the saints have to do, 'works of service', with the final aim of this work of the saints being 'so that the body of Christ may be built up'. It is through the church leadership, the loving service of the saints, that the Body of Christ is to be gathered and built up. Pastors and teachers are given to perfect the saints for this work of church leadership.

A teacher training college is very different from an ordinary school. It seeks not only to train every student to acquire and possess knowledge for him of herself, but to impart it to others. Each congregation is meant to be a training class. Every believer, without exception, is to be thoroughly prepared for the work of the church and taking their part in labour and prayer for those near and far. In all the local church leader's teaching of repentance and conversion, of obedience and holiness, this ought definitely to be their ultimate aim – to call men and women to come and serve God in the noble, holy, Christ-like work of saving the lost and restoring God's Kingdom on earth. The chief end of the church is of necessity the chief end of the ministry.

Out of this follows, naturally, the statement that the chief aim of preaching ought to be to train every believer and every congregation to take its part in helping the church fulfil her destiny. This will decide the question as to how often a mission sermon ought to be preached. As long as only one mission message a year is given, it is possible that the chief thought will be the obtaining of a better collection. This may often be obtained without the spiritual life being raised at all. When global mission takes the true place as the chief purpose of the church, the leader may feel the need, time after time, to return to the one subject, until the neglected truth begins to master at least some in the congregation. At times it may be that while there is no direct preaching on global mission, yet all the teaching on love and faith, on obedience and service, on holiness and conformity to Christ, may be inspired by this one truth – that we are to be 'imitators of God, therefore, as dearly loved children and live a life of love, just as Christ

loved us and gave himself up for us as a fragrant offering
and sacrifice to God' (Eph. 5:1–2).

Leadership training

In view of the responsibility of the church leader, the chief
aim of every church leader ought to be to prepare for this
great work. To become a teacher you need special training. To inspire and train and help believers is not easy; it
does not come from the mere fact that one is an earnest
Christian and has had church leadership training. It is a
matter of giving much larger place to global mission in our
theological seminaries and colleges. But even this can only
be partial and preparatory. The church leader needs to
prepare him or herself successfully to combat the selfishness that is content with personal salvation, the worldliness that has no idea of sacrificing all or even anything for
Christ, the unbelief that measures its power to help or
bless by what it feels and sees. Without doubt he or she
will need special training to fit global mission for this, the
highest and holiest part of his or her calling as a local
church leader.

How can the church leader prepare for carrying out his
or her responsibility? The first answer will usually be by
study.

How often, in the study of the Bible or theology, everything is simply regarded as a matter of the intellect, leaving the heart unchanged. It is possible for someone to
study and know the theory and history of global mission
and yet lack the inspiration that knowledge was meant to
give. To study science with wonder, reverence and humility is a great gift: how much more is all this needed in the
higher area of the spiritual world, and especially in this,
the highest destiny of the church.

To study global mission, we need a deep humility that is conscious of its ignorance, and has no confidence in its own understanding; reverent waiting and patience that is willing to listen to what God's Spirit can reveal; and love and devotion that allows itself to be mastered and led by divine love wherever he leads.

And what is it that a church leader will need especially to study? In the challenge of global mission there are three great factors: the world; Christ and his sacrificial grace; and the church as the link between the two.

The world

Take some of the statistics that tell of the world's population. Think, for instance, of the millions of unevangelised, unreached; take a book that brings you face to face with the situation and often the degradation and suffering of a particular country. Study its diagrams, its maps and its statistics. Stop and ask yourself whether you believe, whether you feel, what you have read. Pause and meditate and pray, asking God to give you an eye to see and a heart to feel that misery. Think of these millions as your fellow human beings.[1]

Look at that picture of a man worshipping a cobra cut in stone with a reverence of which many Christians know little. Take in what it means until you cannot forget it. That man is your brother. He has, like you, a nature formed for worship. He does not, like you, know the true God. Will you not sacrifice everything, even yourself, to be a living witness before him?

Study the state of the world, sometimes in its great whole, sometimes in its detail, until you begin to feel that God has placed you in this dark world with the one object

---

[1] Today we have materials readily available to help us in this exercise. One excellent resource is *Operation World*.

of studying that darkness, and living and helping those who are dying in it.

If at times you feel that it is more than you can bear, cry to God to help you to look again, and again, until you know the need of the world. But remember always that the strongest intellect, the most vivid imagination, the most earnest study, cannot give you the right understanding of these things. Nothing but the Spirit and love of Jesus can make you feel what he feels and love as he loves.

Christ in his love and power

Then comes the second great lesson: Christ's love, dying for sinners, and now longing to have them won for him. Do not think you already know that dying love, that love resting on and thirsting for every creature on earth! If you would study the challenge of global mission, study it in the heart of Jesus. The challenge of global mission is very personal – it applies to every believer. But it is especially true of the church leader who is to be the pattern and the teacher of believers. Study, experience and prove the power of the personal relationship, so that you may be able to teach well this deepest secret of true mission work.

Then with Christ's love there is his power. Study this until the vision of a triumphant Christ, with every enemy at his feet, has cast its light upon the whole earth. The whole work of being a living witness is Christ's work, as much today as on Calvary, as much with each individual conversion as in the propitiation for the sins of all. His divine power carries on the work in and through his servants. In studying the possible solution of the problem, in any case of special difficulty, beware of leaving out the omnipotence of Jesus. Humbly, reverently and patiently worship him, until Christ's love and power become the inspiration of your life.

The church as the link

The third great lesson to study is that of the church, the connecting link between the grace-filled Saviour and the graceless world. Here some of the deepest mysteries of the challenge of global mission will be found:

- That the church should really be the Body of Christ on earth, with the head in heaven, as indispensable to him as he is to it.
- That his omnipotence and his infinite redeeming love should have linked himself, for the fulfilment of his desires, to the weakness of his church.
- That the church should now these many years have heard the declaration, global mission the supreme end of the church, and yet be content with such a poor achievement.
- That the Lord should yet be waiting to prove most wonderfully how really he counts his church one with himself, and is ready to fill her with his Spirit, power and glory.
- That there is abundant ground for a confident faith that the Lord is able and waiting to restore the church to her Pentecost state, and so fit her for carrying out her Pentecost commission.

In the midst of such study there will grow the clearer conviction of how the church is his Body, with the power of his Spirit, true partaker of his divine love, the blessed partner of his life and his glory. Such faith will be awakened if the church will arise and give herself wholly to her Lord.

The world in its sin; Christ in his love and power; the church as the link between the two – these are the three great magnitudes the church leader must know if he or she is to master the challenge of global mission. In study he or she may go to Scripture, to mission literature and to books on theology or the spiritual life; but in the long run he or she will always have to come back to the truth: the problem is a personal one.

It demands a complete and unreserved giving up of the whole being to live for that world, for that Christ, for that church. The living Christ can manifest himself through us; he can impart his love in power. He can make his love ours, so that we may feel as he does. He can let the light of his love fall on the world to reveal its need and its hope. He can give the experience of how close and how real his union is with the believer and how divinely he can dwell and work in us.

The challenge of global mission is a personal one, to be solved by the power of Christ's love. The church leader must study it, so they will learn to preach in new power – global mission, the great work, the supreme end, of Christ, of the church, of every congregation, of every believer, and especially of every church leader.

We have said that the first need of ministry, if it is to fulfil the calling to global mission, is to study global mission. But when light begins to come and the mind is convinced and the emotions are stirred these must immediately be translated into action if they are not to remain barren. And where shall this action begin? Undoubtedly in prayer, more definitely prayer for global mission. It may be for the awakening of the mission spirit in the church at large, or in individual local churches. It may be for some special ministry. It may be, it must be, that God would give and ever renew the mission fire from heaven. Whatever the prayer may be, the study must lead at once to more prayer, or the fruit will be comparatively small. Without prayer, even though there may be increased interest in global mission, more work for global mission, better success in organisation and greater finances, the real growth of the spiritual life and of the love of Christ in the people may be very small.

When our will and work are in the foreground, the spiritual life is weak; God's presence and power are little known. You may have people who read books on mission and faithfully give, yet express little love to Christ or prayer for his Kingdom. You may, on the other hand, have humble, simple people who can give very little, but with that little they give their whole hearts' love and prayer. The latter is on a higher and more spiritual level, in which the love of God is the supreme aim. No one needs to watch more carefully than the church leader to see that the enthusiasm for global mission he fosters in the church leader and others is the fire that comes from heaven in answer to believing prayer to consume the sacrifice.

The challenge of global mission is a personal one. The church leader who has solved it for him of herself will also be able to lead others to find its solution in the constraining power of Christ's love.

12

A Call To Prayer

Introduction

In 1948, on the Isle of Lewis in the Outer Hebrides, a group of church elders met together to pray regularly for God to move among them, their church and the community. On one evening an elder began the meeting with a reading from Psalm 24:

> Who may ascend the hill of the Lord? Who may stand in his holy place? He who has clean hands and a pure heart, who does not lift up his soul to an idol or swear by what is false. He will receive blessing from the Lord and vindication from God his Saviour. Such is the generation of those who seek him, who seek your face, O God of Jacob (Ps. 24:3–6).

The elder then stopped reading, faced the small group and asked, 'Are our hands clean, are our hearts pure?' For hours they prayed and sought forgiveness from God for their own sin; they prayed for each member to know the holiness and purity of God; and they prayed for their community that it would know God.

Within weeks God visited the Isle in a spiritual awakening where many turned to Christ and many sought a deeper spiritual life. Duncan Campbell, who was part of the spiritual awakening, but not part of the prayer meeting, said some time later that the awakening began that night. He later said to a group of young Missionaries with Youth With A Mission, 'A God-sent spiritual awakening must be related to heart purity.'

Throughout his response to the Ecumenical Missionary Conference, which was the background to Andrew Murray's book, there has been a gradual building and challenging to prayer and action for global mission. Now in the closing chapter he openly shares his heart and concern in full crescendo. Here we have a respected and renowned international Christian leader and local church fellowship pastor pleading with his fellow ministers to lead the church in wholehearted prayer and repentance. He asks them to carry this burden for global mission along with him and together to take up the challenge.

> Should we local church leaders not seek with our people to come under the deep conviction that we have not given ourselves to Christ with total devotion; that we have not sufficiently renounced our own interests and ease, and the spirit of the world, to carry out his great command with all our strength?
>
> *Why* should we do this? *Because our heart and life have not been wholly yielded to the transforming power of Christ's spirit and love.*

As you read his words and his heart, allow them to penetrate, and ask 'What, Lord, do you require of me?'

* * * * *

A Call to Prayer

Over the previous pages I have frequently spoken of prayer. As I come to the closing chapter, I feel that all that has been said will profit little unless it leads to prayer. As we look at the extent of the need for global mission and the greatness of the work that still has to be done; at the utterly inadequate workforce that the church has at present sent out in the world as living witnesses, we are crushed. We do not see sufficient signs that she is ready yet to place herself and all her resources at her Lord's disposal. We see our absolute powerlessness to give life either in the church locally or globally and weakness in our dependence upon the power that comes in answer to prayer and faith. We are amazed at the love of our Lord to his people and to the lost, and the promises he waits to fulfil. We feel that our only hope is to apply ourselves to prayer.

Prayer, more prayer, much prayer, very special prayer, should first of all be made for the work to be done in our local churches on behalf of global mission. That is indeed the one great need of the day.

To whom do we call?

'My help comes from the Lord, the Maker of heaven and earth' (Ps. 121:2). If these words are true, and they certainly are the very truth of God, surely the first concern for leaders in churches and mission agencies, to whom the spiritual training of their members is entrusted by God, should be to give prayer the same place that it has in the purpose of God.

To quote again from the Ecumenical Missionary Conference of 1900, Revd W. Perkins declared:

> The global mission movement was born in prayer. Prayer is the vital breath by which it lives. Great are the results are of global mission, but they would have been a hundredfold greater if the Church of Christ had been what she ought to be in the two great matters of prayer and giving.
>
> What is needed is that the spiritual life of every Christian, and so of the whole Church, should be so deepened, instructed and inspired by the Holy Spirit that it shall

become as natural and easy to pray daily for global mission as to pray for daily bread. The Church must develop the conviction that the law of sacrifice is the law of life. We must find time for prayer, even though it may mean withholding time from pleasure and business. Only sacrifice is fruitful.

There must be developed in the Church by the Spirit of God a penetrating and abiding sense of the world's urgent need, its misery, darkness and despair. A power must come that shall make the need so real, so terrible, that our first feeling shall be one of helplessness in the face of it; our next feeling, 'I must go and pray about it'; and the next, 'I will give up and sacrifice even necessities, in the presence of conditions like these for which Christ died.

If these words are to be taken seriously and do any good, the great question is, surely, how are our leaders to awaken and to train the churches to that life of prayer of which they speak? Since there are many who give but do not pray, or give little and pray little, those who know what prayer is must pray and labour more earnestly. Let them pray that the life of Christians may be so deepened by the Holy Spirit that it shall become 'as natural and easy to pray daily for global mission as to pray for daily bread'. God can do it. Let it be our definite aim and prayer – God will do it!

All evangelical teaching acknowledges the work of the Holy Spirit and the power of prayer to secure his working. Yet it is only when they have *first place* and everything else is made subordinate to them that the Christian life will be truly healthy.

Of all the questions claiming the concern of the leaders of our local churches, there is not one that demands more urgent consideration, that is more difficult to decide, and that will bring a richer reward, than this: how can the church be educated to more persistent, fervent, believing prayer?

Prayer will at once be the means and the proof of stronger Christian life, or more devotion to Christ's service, and of the blessing of heaven descending on our work. Much prayer would be the sign that we had found again the path by which the early church entered on its triumphant course.

We cannot teach people to pray just by telling them to do so. Prayer is the pulse of the life. The call to more prayer must be connected with the deepening of spiritual life. As we have seen from the life and experiences of Hudson Taylor, the two great conditions of true prayer are an urgent sense of need and a full assurance of a supply for that need. We must bring God's children to see and feel the need. The work entrusted to them; the obligation to do it; the consequence to ourselves, to Christ, to the perishing, of neglecting it; our absolute powerlessness to do it in our own strength – these great truths must master us.

On the other side, the love of Christ to us and to the world; our access to God in him as Intercessor; the certainty of persevering prayer being heard; the blessedness of a life of prayer; the blessings it can bring to the world – these, too, must grip us.

We must learn to pray in secret, to wait on God, to take hold of his strength. We must teach Christians to pray in little groups, with the joy and the love and the faith that fellowship brings. We must gather the whole church in special times of prayer, when his power will work above what we can ask or think.

Prayer and remorse

In the heading of this chapter I have spoken of prayer and remorse. By remorse I mean prayer that is filled with contrition, repentance and penitence. Frequently mentioned are the shortcomings of church leaders, in interest and prayer and giving, of the failure of the church as a whole to do her duty. And yet where is the solemnity, the awesome loss of neglect to the Lord's commission? Do we realise the terrible sin of disobedience?

There is an optimism around that loves to speak of what is bright and hopeful. It believes that in doing so thanks are brought to God and courage to his servants. Above everything it is afraid of pessimism. And yet optimism and pessimism are errors equally to be avoided. Each is one-sided; they are both extremes. Experience teaches us that, when we have to deal with two apparently conflicting truths, there is only one way to see the true relation. We should look first to the one as if it were all, and thoroughly master all that it means. Then turn to the other, and grasp as fully all that it implies. When we know both, we are in a position to walk in the centre of the path of truth.

Applying this to missions

On the one side there is so much to rejoice in, to thank God for and to take courage from. Surely we never can give God too much praise for what he has done during the past century. On the other hand, there is so much work that has not been done that could have been done, for the reason that the church was not what she ought to be. Millions still are without the knowledge of Christ, and will go on perishing, simply because the church is not doing the work for which she was redeemed and endowed with God's Spirit.

When we are brought face to face with this truth, our hearts will spontaneously cry out in remorse, repentance and shame. We will confess our sins. What sins are we committing?

- The sin of disobedience and unbelief.
- The sin of selfishness and worldliness, grieving the Holy Spirit and quenching Christ's love in our hearts.
- The sin of not living utterly for Christ, for his love and his Kingdom.

These sins will become a burden greater than we can bear until we have laid them at our Lord's feet and seen him remove them.

In Scripture we find men who were most jealous for the honour of God, most diligent in his service, and least guilty of sin, were the first to confess it and mourn over it. Moses, David, Ezra, Nehemiah and Daniel were the Godliest men of their times and were the men most conscious of sin.

Is the sin of the majority of members to be counted as the sin of the whole Body? I am speaking of the most devoted friends of Christ and of global mission – the leaders who in the church or in mission agencies, as supporters, mission workers or mobilisers. These are people who, by virtue of their spiritual insight, ought to feel the sin most, to carry it to God, and then to appeal to others to come and join them in repentance and confession.

We spoke of the need of a new Pentecost era; it must be preceded by great repentance and turning from sin. This will not happen until the leaders, to whom the Lord gives the deepest sense of the sin of his people, have gathered them with a call to repentance and surrender to full obedience. The appeal to global mission gives us one of the grandest opportunities for repentance as it uncovers the sins that lie at the root.

This has always been God's way: remorse and repentance precedes restoration and renewal. On the day of Pentecost it was the preaching of 'God has made this Jesus, whom you crucified both Lord and Christ'

(Acts 2:36) that broke hearts and prepared them for the receiving of the Holy Spirit. We still need the same kind of preaching to God's people. If we are to summon Christians to a life of higher devotion in God's service, the wrong, the shame, the guilt of our present state must be set before them.

It is when sin is felt and confessed that Christ's pardoning love will be felt afresh. That new experience of his power and love will become the incentive to make that love known to others. It is the repentant heart that God makes alive. It is to the humbled soul that he gives more grace. An essential element in a true spiritual awakening will be a broken heart and a contrite spirit in view of past neglect and sin over global mission.

This preaching of remorse on account of our lack of obedience to Christ's great command will be no easy thing. It will need men and women who wait before God for the vision of what this sin of the church really implies. Hudson Taylor spent five years in China feeling its darkness without grasping its full significance. He spent five more years in England working and praying for China; he still did not know how great its awful need was. Only when he began to prepare a statement for publication on China's needs did he feel the full horror of the thick darkness. He could find no rest until God gave him the twenty-four workers he had prayed for, and he was willing to accept the responsibility to lead them out. Similarly we shall require men and women who give themselves, in study and prayer and love, to take in all the terrible meaning of the words we utter so easily – that the church is disobedient to her Lord's last and greatest command.

In such prayer and remorse the church leaders must take the lead. The preaching of prayer and remorse cannot be in power if the church leader has no experience of it. The challenge of mission is a personal one – for the church leaders, too. Both on their own behalf and as representatives of the people, they must take the lead.

> Let the priests, who minister before the Lord, weep between the temple porch and the altar. Let them say, 'Spare your people, O Lord. Do not make your inheritance an object of scorn, a byword among the nations. Why should they say among the peoples, "Where is their God?"' (Joel 2:17).

Is there any one church of which it can be said that the extension of Christ's Kingdom is the one goal for which it lives? Do not all admit that the church is not what she should be? Is it not plain that, if this continues, the evangelisation of the world will be impossible?

With the church as a whole so guilty before God, should not every minister take some part of the blame for this condition?

Should we local church leaders not seek with our people to come under the deep conviction that we have not given ourselves to Christ with total devotion; that we have not sufficiently renounced our own interests and ease, and the spirit of the world, to carry out his great command with all our strength?

Why should we do this? Because our hearts and lives have not been wholly yielded to the transforming power of Christ's spirit and love.

Although we all in some degree share this responsibility, there is no possible way for the ministry to remove the evil and promote a better state without every one of us confessing our lack of that enthusiastic love to Christ which would have enabled us to be true witnesses to him. When such a spirit of repentance takes hold of the ministry, there will be hope for the people. If in public preaching and praying the tone of repentance and confession is clear and deep, there will surely be a response in the hearts of all earnest people. Those who are now our best contributors will feel how much more God asks – and is willing to give, through his Holy Spirit – of fervent love and prevailing prayer, and full consecration of all to his service. It will be proved in our mission work: 'Everyone who exalts himself will be humbled, and he who humbles himself will be exalted' (Lk. 14:11).

Repentance is always the gate to larger blessing. What did he who holds the seven stars in his right hand say to the church of Ephesus?

> I know your deeds, your hard work and your perseverance. I know that you cannot tolerate wicked men, that you have tested those who claim to be apostles but are not, and have found them false. You have persevered and have endured hardships for my name, and have not grown weary (Rev. 2:2–3).

This certainly seemed to be a model church. What diligence and zeal in good works; what patience in suffering; what purity in discipline; what zeal for orthodoxy; and what unwearied perseverance in it all. And best of all, it was for his name's sake. And yet the Lord was not satisfied.

> Yet I hold this against you: You have forsaken your first love. Remember the height from which you have fallen! Repent and do the things you did at first. If you do not repent, I will come to you and remove your lamp stand from its place' (Rev. 2:4–5).

The loss our first love

The tenderness and fervour of personal attachment to the Lord Jesus was now lacking. Their works were still being done in his name, but they were no longer like the first works, in the spirit of their first love. He calls them to contrition and remorse: he calls them to look back, repent and do the first works. It is possible to work much and earnestly for Christ and his cause in commendable ways as far as anyone can judge; but there may be lacking that without which the works are as nothing in his sight.

He counts the love of personal attachment to Christ as the love the greatest of all. God is Love. Christ loved us and gave himself. His love was a tender, holy giving of himself, a personal friendship and fellowship. That love of his, cherished in the heart in daily close communion, responded to by a love that clings to him, proved by his love pervading all our labour for others – it is that which makes our work acceptable. It was this first love to Christ that gave the early church its power. It was this Pentecost love that Christ calls them to remember, from which they were fallen, and to which, in repentance, they were to return. Nothing less can satisfy the heart of him who loved us. Shall we not give it to him?

It is this early church Pentecost love to which we must return in our mission work – local and global. We have seen how God made the Moravian Church the first church of the Reformation to take the early church Pentecost stand and give her wholly to bringing the gospel to every creature. We have seen that it was love – a passionate, adoring contemplation of Christ's dying love, a passionate desire to make that love known. That was the key. Global mission was the automatic outflow and overflow of their love for Christ. It was to satisfy Christ's love and express their own love that they brought to him people that he had died to save. That made the most insignificant of churches the greatest of all.

As we mourn over the state of the church today, with all its unfaithfulness to Christ and to the perishing of the unreached, let us, above all, make confession of the loss of our first love.

'Do you love me?'

Do you remember how even Peter, after his fall from his first love, could not be restored till the searching question 'Do you truly love me?' (Jn. 21:15) had deeply wounded him? Then he penitently, but confidently, answered, 'Yes Lord ... you know that I love you' (Jn. 21:15).

As we repent and mourn the past, let us press on to wait before our Lord with the one prayer:

> Love, Lord! It is your love we need.
> We know about it; we have preached it; we have sought to find it.
> We wait in humility and reverence and wonder before you.
> O Loving One, shed that love abroad in our hearts by your Holy Spirit.
> We look to you to enable us in the power of that love to take the world into our hearts.
> Like Jesus, we want to live and die only that his love may triumph over every human being!

Part III

Developing A Mission Lifestyle

Introduction

We have spent some considerable time looking at what a Mission Lifestyle is and how individuals and whole communities of believers, the church, should be developing in one. After all, as Murray would say, the challenge of global mission is a personal one for every believer in every local church. So how do we begin developing in practical ways a Mission Lifestyle, as individuals and as local fellowships?

It was with this question ringing in our ears and buzzing around our minds that Greg Reader and I set time apart to begin thinking this through in more detail during the summer of 2000. The materials we developed formed part of the programme for the European MISSION Congress at the end of that year. Since then they have been used in different places and in different situations in Europe. Greg has used them in various training situations with International Teams, particularly in the Philippines. Part III, then, is a compilation of our thinking and writing.

These materials are designed not only for the individual thinking of developing a Mission Lifestyle, but whole groups and communities of believers. They can be adapted for small group, cell-based study, or for one-on-one mentoring relationships. I have discovered that church leaders have found them useful as they assist in their ongoing understanding of and relationships with people who enter into cross-cultural mission activity, whether short or long term.

The first chapter in this section takes up the challenge from Andrew Murray and builds upon his suggestion for developing prayer for global mission. It is based upon the prayer framework given by Murray in his original book, *The Key to the Missionary Problem*. At Murray's time this was used extensively around the world.

From here we will begin to construct a Mission Lifestyle development plan by forming a personal profile. This can form the basis for areas of action, personal development or group discipleship. Remember that one challenge of a Mission Lifestyle is to think globally, act locally. Therefore this raises a set of questions that need investigating, focused around the question of what is happening in the locality. How many cultures are present and are spiritual needs being met across cultural barriers in the locality?

As these questions are raised, some people will ask more personal questions, such as 'Am I in the right locality?' or 'Does God want me to move into a different culture or country?' Another integral part of a Mission Lifestyle is being involved in sending people into other contexts and communities around the world.

13

Week Of Prayer For Global Mission

The starting place for developing a Mission Lifestyle is prayer.

The following week-long prayer calendar has been adapted from the suggested week of prayer given by Andrew Murray. This original prayer framework went on to set the agenda for the annual Evangelical Alliance's World Week of Prayer, which takes place still during early January.

Each day for a week, beginning on a Sunday and ending the following Sunday, follow and pray through the prayer framework. On some of the days you are directed to particular points for intercession, while on others you will be inspired to prayerful meditation and to confession and repentance. Throughout the week of prayer allow God to speak to you concerning development of the Mission Lifestyle in your own life and in the life of the group of local believers you belong to.

First day

Praise

Read Psalm 145:11–13.

> Praise God for:
> the glory of his Kingdom in the earth
> what he has accomplished
> the share he gives us in his work
> what he is doing and is going to do.

Read 2 Chronicles 20:14–22.

Second day

The work

Read 2 Corinthians 2:16.

> Read the opening chapter of *Operation World*, which gives a
> brief assessment of world evangelisation and the extent of
> the task we face.
> Use this information in prayer. Also include in your prayers:
> the difficulty of the work and the power of Satan (Eph. 6:12)
> the urgency of the task.

The workers

Read Philippians 2:15–16.

> Pray for:
> the church
> the Body of Christ
> that all members, without exception, would realise they are
> redeemed to take part in the work.

Pray for a vision of:
the need of the world
the glory of Christ
the calling of believers

Pray for those you know who at this time have set aside time to work full-time in this cause.

Read Colossians 4:2–4.

Third day

The Holy Spirit

Read 1 Corinthians 12:6.

All mission work is God's own work and the Holy Spirit is the mighty power of God working in us.

The Spirit was given at Pentecost as the power to bring the gospel to every person (Jn. 15:26–27; Acts 1:8).

All failure is owing to the loss of this power (Gal. 3:3).

All genuine global mission work of giving, praying and working is only of value if the power of the Spirit is in it (Rom. 15:16).

Our prayer and God's promise of the Spirit meeting us is the only hope for our participation in global mission being successful (Acts 4:31).

Pray for the power of the Spirit:
as the enthusiasm of Christ's presence and love in the church
in mission agencies
in your own congregation
in your own life
with the one aim of witnessing of Jesus to every human being.

Read Luke 24:47.

Fourth day

Confession

Read Psalm 51.

> Confess:
> the failure of the church to know and fulfil her mission
> the lack of entire consecration to Christ's honour and
> Kingdom
> the lack of love and self-sacrifice in giving and praying
> (Hag. 1:11; Mal. 3:10; Phil. 2:21)
>
> Repentance is the only path to restoration (Is. 58:1–2, 6–7;
> Gen. 42:21).
>
> Pray for the Spirit to convince you and the church of sin.

Read 1 John 1:5–10.

Fifth day

Prayer

Read Matthew 6:5–15.

> Prayer is the chief factor on humankind's side in doing God's
> work, it is the key to all heavenly blessing and power
> (Lk. 11:13; Jn. 14:13–14; Eph. 3:20).
>
> The difficulty of prayer is that it needs the crucifixion of self
> to strive, labour and agonise, in order that we watch in
> prayer (Rom. 15:30; Col. 4:12).
>
> Prayer needs a spiritual mind to delight in fellowship with
> Christ, and to believe that our prayers will prevail.

The urgent necessity of prayer for global mission is that more believers are involved and more money is supplied. But the need of more prayer, such as ushered in Pentecost, is greater.

Pray that in this week of prayer God may give us the spirit of prayer; that there may be a great increase of secret, habitual, fervent, believing intercession for the power of the Spirit in all our global mission work.

Read John 17:1–5.

Sixth day

Consecration

Read 2 Chr. 7:14.

If confession has been real, if prayer has been honest, there must follow a new surrender (2 Chr. 15:8–15).

This implies a turning away from all sin and from all short-comings to a life of entire obedience and devotion (2 Cor. 5:15).

It implies especially a very personal giving of one's self to the Lord Jesus and his love, to be kept by him and used, as his own property and possession (2 Tim. 2:21; Tit. 2:14).

Everything depends on this: the challenge of global mission is a personal one.

Explicitly implied is that we serve Christ by seeking and serving people who do not know him. Concern for global mission is expressed in interest; giving financially; praying; fellowship with others; and also in making him known to those around us.

Pray for your place in this.

Read John 17:20–26.

Seventh day

Faith

Read 1 Peter 3:8–12.

The power in humankind that corresponds to the power of God is the power that leads to prayer, grows strong in prayer, and prevails in prayer (Mk. 11:24). It is the power that overcomes the world, because Christ has overcome it, and faith that lives in union with him (Jn. 16:33; 1 Jn. 5:4, 5).

Missions have no foundation or law but in God's purpose, God's promise, God's power. These divine possibilities are the food of faith, and call every mission friend to this one thing – to be strong in faith, giving glory to God.

Pray that this week may lead to:
a deep revelation of God's readiness and power to fulfil in us the promises he made to his people
a great quickening of true faith in every mission worker and helper at home and abroad.

Read Matthew 28:18–20.

Final day

The love of Christ

Read Romans 8:31.

Our aim is that the love of Christ is to triumph in every human heart (Phil. 2:13).

This should be our only desire and its possession our only power for being living witnesses (2 Cor. 5:14).

Let us once more saturate our spirits with the Moravian motivation and participation in global mission:

Get this burning thought of 'personal love for the Saviour who redeemed me' into the hearts of all Christians, and you have the most powerful incentive for the global mission effort.

If we could make this a personal one goal and target; if we could fill the hearts of the people with a personal love for the Saviour who died for them; then the indifference of the church would disappear and the Kingdom of Christ would appear.

Read Revelation 5:6–10.

14

The Mission Lifestyle Profile

Paul, in his letter to the Philippians, writes that he rejoiced whenever he remembered them. He then writes:

> There has never been the slightest doubt in my mind that the God who started this great work in you would keep at it and bring it to a flourishing finish on the very day Christ Jesus appears (Phil. 1:6, MSG).

In other words, discovery of God and the challenges and changes that follow constitute a life-long journey.

Change can be both exciting and also painful. Look at your life and walk with God and how he has begun to change you. This process will continue throughout your life.

We have seen how being involved in mission is not an optional extra for any Christian. It's our mandate, our lifestyle. If you count yourself a Christian, then you are to be part of mission: the people of God going to the people of the world.

In the book *How to be a World Class Christian* Paul Borthwick describes such people as 'World Christians', whose 'lifestyle and obedience are compatible, in co-operation and in accord with what God is doing and wants to do in our world'.[1] Meanwhile, we have seen that

---

[1] Paul Borthwick, *How to be a World Class Christian: You can be a Part of God's Global Action* (OM, 1999), p. 24.

Andrew Murray encourages us to be living witnesses in the world, and together these descriptions help us to see how we are to develop a Mission Lifestyle.

The above are not descriptions of some elite form of Christian, because in just the same way as all believers are caught up in mission, so all are called to be world Christians, living witnesses forming and growing in a Mission Lifestyle. We are to be day-to-day disciples who take Christ's global cause to be the integrating, overriding priority. Like disciples should, we actively investigate all that the Great Commission means and become participators in it. God wants the hearts and minds of Christians to be in pace with his will and purposes for the world.

In this chapter, with the aid of the Mission Lifestyle Profile, we are going to look at developing such a lifestyle. Like other areas of discipleship, its development is an ongoing process.

The Mission Lifestyle Profile explained

The Mission Lifestyle Profile exercise has been designed to help you to begin to build up a picture of your own Mission Lifestyle. It will help you identify your strengths as well as areas for development and action. There are no right or wrong answers in the profile, and hopefully no trick questions either. It has been designed simply for you to do an audit to discover where you are and to point to where you want to be in each area.

The profile can be used individually or in a fellowship group or cell setting. If you are in a mentoring or close discipleship relationship, the profile is also very useful to assess current and future desires and development. It is often beneficial for the mentor also to complete Step 1 on those he or she is discipling, as this adds dimension of 'how others see us' into the discussion.

Completing the Mission Lifestyle Profile

The profile is in two parts. Step 1 is a questionnaire and Step 2 is a worksheet. In each, take your time in answering, and give clear, honest answers.

Step 1

Take your time to read and assess each statement to determine which best describes you at the present time.

Step 2

Now turn to the Mission Lifestyle Worksheet. Using your own words, explain the statement you chose in the Profile and write what action you think you need to take.

What next?

After completing Steps 1 and 2 of the Mission Lifestyle Profile you should have a clearer idea of how you are developing your Mission Lifestyle and which areas you want to improve or explore.

If you are part of a small group whose members are looking at this together, discuss what similarities and differences there are between you. Remember that there are no right or wrong answers and that each person may be thinking and being led by God in different ways, so affirm each person's uniqueness and give thanks for the way God is leading each of you. Discussing together, you will begin to build up a picture of your community Mission Lifestyle. As part of these discussions, decide what action points you could work on together.

If you are studying alone, then look at your action points and prioritise them in the order you would like to approach and explore them.

Mission Lifestyle Profile

Step 1

Read the following statements and, selecting one from each row, mark that which best applies to you.

Spiritual Maturity	Accepts God's love and forgiveness	Is being increasingly changed by God's spirit. More love, joy, peace, patience, gentleness, self-control	Is growing in the use of spiritual gifts and disciplines, especially prayer and Bible study	Is growing in personal and corporate worship	Lifestyle is increasingly shaped by biblical standards	A growing understanding of God's biblical purposes for the whole world and of their role in this
Married Identity	Practises mutual submission and loving service	Freely expresses feelings	Seeks to resolve conflicts	Good balance between work, rest and recreation. Protects time for the family	Children are nurtured and trained lovingly. Each family member is encouraged in spiritual and ministry growth	Relates well to the larger community
Single Identity	Accepts single status	Freely expresses feelings	Seeks to resolve conflicts	Good balance between work, rest and recreation	Aware of particular challenges of being single in various contexts	Relates well to the larger community
Servant's Heart	Increasingly moved with compassion for others	Submits to Christ's Lordship in trust and obedience	Doesn't put self over others	Serves others with diligence, faithfulness, and joy	Follows through on commitments made in response to God's guidance	Models to others Christ's humility, forgiveness and mercy
Adaptability	Finds security in God's sovereignty	Is not threatened by diversity. Distinguishes between what's wrong and what's just different	Adapts well to new situations	Appreciates various personalities and styles of leadership	Copes well in difficult circumstances	Is committed to life-long learning

Cultural Sensitivity	Appreciates and values different cultures	Has a growing ability to see things from others' perspectives. Is sensitive to his or her expectations and values	Has a growing understanding of his or her own cultural filters	Is willing to learn another person's language	Can adapt to differences in models of learning and leading and to standards of living and technology	Can adapt to differences in humour and laugh at self
Church	Is actively involved in local church life	Reflects Christ's love by serving the church	Values the diversity of the church	Sacrificially resources mission	Challenges and disciples others to participate in mission	Promotes the synergy of global and local mission
Bible Study	Uses various study methods effectively	Can understand and apply Scripture. Interprets passages in the light of their biblical context	Grasps the biblical story and its missionary nature	Can discern between major and minor biblical emphases	Can identify and express biblical doctrines, themes and principles	Is able to assist others to study the Bible effectively
Evangelism	Shares Christ in culturally appropriate ways	Can communicate clearly what Christ has done in his or her own life	Leads people to Christ and into the Christian community	Lives out and explains the gospel	Does not separate 'word and deed' in the task of evangelism	Can equip others to communicate the gospel effectively
Discipleship	Teaches new believers the basics of the faith	Helps others to grow in spiritual maturity and ministry skills	Forms mutual accountability relationships	Is accessible and supportive to others	Helps others to identify and develop their spiritual gifts	Mentors and releases others to be active in mission
Leadership	Can formulate and communicate compelling vision	Plans and organises effectively	Empowers by appropriate delegation and celebrates others' contributions	Identifies, nurtures and equips potential leaders	Navigates conflict and crisis well	Learns through listening and observing
Relationship	Is able to listen and communicate effectively	Builds trust with others	Can identify and work well with people of different temperaments	Relates appropriately to men/women	Understand and appreciates different perspectives	Contributes to the resolution of conflict, emphasising forgiveness and reconciliation

Learning	Knows his or her best learning style	Is following a plan for personal development in every area of life. Has a strong biblical theology of vocation	Makes use of the full spectrum of resources and learning available	Seeks the challenge of other perspectives	Can discern and assess the implications of current trends for his or her ministry	Regularly evaluates his or her own relevance and competence
Learning Another Language	Picks up words and phrases from other languages	Discerns and is able to form sounds not native to his or her mother tongue	Discerns grammatical structures and patterns	Perseveres through long-term, repetitive learning processes. Can keep laughing at him or herself	Uses language in living, learning and ministry	Discerns subtleties in a language such as regional distinctions, humour, etc.
Cultural Adaptation	Enjoys interacting with people from other cultures	Discerns value differences between cultures	Deliberately attempts to look at his or her own culture from the perspective of other cultures	Allows another culture to influence and bring change to his or her attitudes, perspectives and behaviour	Effectively interprets social environments	Identifies with and embraces another culture
Professional	Has adequate professional qualifications for his or her work	Maintains personal and organisational accountability	Manages self effectively; organises work efficiently	Views life as an integrated whole	Understands how his or her particular work is part of mission	Offers his or her work skills in service to others
Simplicity and Stewardship	Views possessions as things God has entrusted to him or her to be used wisely	Tithes regularly	Gives generously to help others	Has chosen not to pursue material gain for its own sake	Is not trapped in debt or encumbered by excessive financial and material concerns	Makes purchasing and other lifestyle choices from a mission perspective rather than a consumer perspective

Mission Lifestyle Worksheet

Step 2

Using your own words, explain the statement you chose in the Mission Lifestyle Profile and write what action you think you need to take.

Spiritual Maturity	Action
Married Identity/Single Identity	Action
Servant's Heart	Action
Adaptability	Action
Cultural Sensitivity	Action

Church	Action
Bible Study	Action
Evangelism	Action
Discipleship	Action
Leadership	Action
Relationship	Action

Learning	Action
Learning another Language	Action
Cultural Adaptation	Action
Professional	Action
Simplicity and Stewardship	Action

15

Developing Cross-Cultural Awareness

Today in Europe there are not many places that are unaffected by pluralism and multi-culturalism. However, often we do not associate with people from others cultures, even when they are on our doorstep. An integral part of a Mission Lifestyle is exposure to, awareness of and service in other cultures.

The following list of questions is designed to help you look at your locality and life differently. Answer honestly and make decisions on actions that are realistic for you. If you studying this as a group, don't only work through and discuss individual answers, but also what actions could be taken as a group.

Cross-Cultural Involvement Worksheet

Question	Action
What ethnic or cultural groups do you live near that are different from your own?	
Have you ever attended worship services of another ethnic group? What were your impressions? How did it broaden your understanding of God?	
What books have you read that describe the differences among cultures? What did you learn?	
How often have you eaten cuisine from other cultures? What types of cuisine do you enjoy the most? Do you deliberately try unfamiliar food?	

Question	Action
Do you enjoy listening to music from other cultures?	
Do you keep up with current events in other parts of the world?	
How do you hear the perspectives of other cultures concerning current events in your country?	
What country or countries would you like to visit?	
Have you ever travelled outside your home country or lived for more than three months in another culture?	
As a Christian, how has your perspective changed by being involved with people from cultures other than your own?	

16

Making Decisions With God's Guidance

Throughout life we have decisions to make. Some are big, life-changing ones, and others are small and inconsequential. However, sometimes the smallest of decisions can be difficult to make. I remember the first time I went to America, the land where everything is twice its usual size – including the decisions.

I arrived, after an exhausting twelve-hour journey, in Colorado Springs and was met by my hosts, Bob and LaRae. On arriving at their home LaRae asked what I wanted to drink. Decision number one was simple, and without hesitation I replied, 'Tea, please.'

The second decision caught me off guard, 'What flavour of tea would I like?' I had not realised that the nation which once threw tea into Boston harbour had managed to replenish its stocks with so many varieties: lemon, raspberry, herb, spice, cinnamon, thyme and forest fruits, among others, were all duly displayed on the kitchen table. In all, I counted twelve varieties, the last of which was English Breakfast Tea. I played safe and opted for this.

However, the assault of decision making was not over yet, as I now had to decide what type of milk I wanted: full fat, half fat, high fat, low fat, raspberry or cinnamon? By this point I was beaten and submerged into culture shock and jet lag. Making too many choices over a simple cup of tea paralysed me. In the end I had it black.

But can God use me?

Of course, not all decision making is like that, but sometimes even the smallest of choices can be difficult. What hope, therefore, do we have when making major decisions? However, often one question needs to be addressed before asking 'What I do' is 'Can God use me?'

Throughout human history God has invited people to participate with him in his Kingdom and in making his ways known. He has even been known to use animals, like Balaam's donkey, to give his message. Age, race, gender or economics are not an issue, as you can see by spending time reading the following passages: Judges 16: 26; 1 Samuel 3; Jeremiah 1:4–10.

What is important is that we are in a state of readiness to be used by God at all times. Here is a condensed list that it is useful to keep in mind in order to maintain this state of perpetual readiness.

Firstly, live according to God's Word. The Psalmist in Psalm 119:9 asks the question 'How can a young man keep his way pure?' out of motivation to be available to God for service. The answer given – 'By living according to your word' – is responded to by the youth with the determination to 'seek you with all my heart; do not let me stray from your commands'. Therefore, spend time reading and studying the Bible.

Secondly, live right before other believers. Cultivating a personal faith is one thing, but living in relation to it can be a completely different thing. Paul mentored Timothy not to 'let anyone look down on you because you are young, but set an example for the believers in speech, in life, in love, in faith and in purity' (1 Tim. 4:12).

Thirdly, flee evil desires. Building upon understanding God from Scripture and relating to other believers, we are to pursue righteousness and holiness. Again Paul mentors Timothy in the words 'Flee the evil desires of youth, and pursue righteousness, faith, love, and peace, along with those who call on the Lord our of a pure heart' (2 Tim. 2:22). Elsewhere, he encourages members of the church in Galatia to produce fruits of the Spirit in their lives.

Fourthly, Jesus himself instructs us to be living witnesses to God to those around us and so to become witnesses to the world. Matthew records Jesus' words:

> You are the salt of the earth ... You are the light of the world. A city on a hill cannot be hidden ... let your light shine before men, that they may see you good deeds and praise your Father in heaven' (Mt. 5:13–16).

Finally, we should be filled with the Holy Spirit. Jesus tells his disciples 'you will receive power when the Holy Spirit comes on you; and you will be my witnesses in Jerusalem, Samaria, and to the ends of the earth' (Acts 1:8).

This filling with the Spirit should be continuous filling, not a one-time blessing or experience. A friend of Andrew Murray, Dwight L. Moody, was asked why he thought it important the need to seek continual filling of the Spirit. His answer was short, yet spoke volumes. He replied, 'Because I leak!'

The Holy Spirit's work is to be the 'One who gives encouragement and comfort' (Jn. 14:26). In John's Gospel the personality of the Spirit reaches its peak when the Spirit is spoken of as the one who proceeds from the Father, sent in the name of the Son. The special name John gives to the Spirit is the 'Paraclete'. The Spirit is the one who leads and guides (Jn. 20:22) and who aids worship (Jn. 4:24).

Meanwhile, Paul writes that the Spirit helps believers in their weaknesses (Rom. 8:26); convicts of sin (2 Thes. 2:13); is the one who reveals God (1 Cor. 2:10); gives gifts (Rom. 12:6) and fertilises spiritual growth (Gal. 5:22).

Throughout the Bible, one clear understanding and function of the Holy Spirit is for sure: the Spirit is the one who empowers believers for witnessing (Acts 1:8). When comparing the work of Christ and with the work of the Spirit, A.W. Tozer wrote, 'Christ died for our hearts and the Holy Spirit wants to come and satisfy them.' In other words, the Spirit enables us to put our faith into action and keeps us in a state of readiness to be used by God in global mission.

Object of scale

Making the fundamental decision to embrace a Mission Lifestyle is one thing. Working out the specifics can be quite another.

- What career path should I follow?
- How should I use my spare time and holidays?
- Who should I work alongside?
- What kind of team should I be a part of?
- Should I focus on a particular group or type of people in my witness and service?
- Should I join a Christian organisation? If so, which one? And should it be part time or full time?
- Should I stay where I am, or move to another part of the world?

Sometimes God makes his will crystal clear in a particular situation – but not always. In fact, the ability to make our own decisions is part of the maturity God desires for us. It honours him and brings him joy when his children make wise decisions! Not that we should then attempt to leave him out of the process. He wants us to talk decisions through with him all along the way and to stay open to the possibility of him suddenly saying 'I want you to do this, not that.' But usually, instead of telling us exactly what to do, he helps us to weigh all the factors involved and then leaves the decision to us. Some of the factors that we need to consider are:

Common sense	God expects us to make good use of the minds he has given us. What makes sense in this situation?
Wise counsel from mature believers	What do others advise?
Context	What are the broader implications? How will the decision affect family, friends, community, and so on?
Experience	What lessons have you already learnt which have a bearing on the decision?
Personal desires	What would you rather do? What gets you excited and motivated? What doesn't?
Temperament	What type of personality do you have? Are you an extrovert? Introvert? Adventurous? Conservative? Do you have high energy levels?
Capabilities	What are your gifts and skills? Are they suited to what you want to do?
Scripture	What principles from Scripture apply?

Prayer	are you talking all of this through with God, asking him for wisdom and expressing your willingness to obey if he gives you specific guidance?
God's specific leading	is God saying anything in particular related to this decision? If so, how is he saying it?

The 'Making Decisions with God's Guidance Worksheet' can help you compare and weigh the factors mentioned above when you need to make a significant decision. You don't need to write something in every box, but spend time considering each section anyway. Unfortunately, you will seldom find that everything you write points in the same direction. For example, two people you trust and respect might give you differing advice, or their advice might not be in tune with what you passionately desire to do. This is where wisdom is needed – it's not a simple matter of adding up all the points for and against! The final decision will lie with you, but it will be a good and God-honouring one if you work through this process while honestly seeking wisdom and guidance from him (Jas. 1:5–6).

Making Decisions With God's Guidance
Worksheet

Description of decision to be made:		
	Pros	Cons
Common sense *What's it telling me?*		
Wise counsel from mature believers *What advice am I getting?*		
Context *How will others be affected?*		
Experience *What have I learnt before?*		
Personal desires *What excites me?* *What doesn't?*		
Temperament *How is my personality suited/unsuited?*		
Capabilities *What relevant gifts and skills do I have?*		

Scripture *What principles apply?*		
Prayer *Are you and others talking this through with God?*		
God's specific leading *Has he said anything?*		

17

What About Short-Term Serving?

Short-term service, if carried out in the right way, should have positive consequences not only for the individual who goes to serve, but also for the local situation he or she serves in and the local church community he or she is from. Together these three beneficiaries should experience growth and development in their collective Mission Lifestyles.

Brandon was hitchhiking home from university when his life was changed. Dave offered him a ride and Brandon climbed in. During the ensuing conversation, Dave shared his testimony with Brandon. Brandon's heart was touched and, a few days later, he put his trust in Christ. He got involved in a small Baptist church and grew in his faith. A couple of years later, Dave and his wife went to Thailand as missionaries. It wasn't long before Brandon was wondering if he shouldn't do something similar.

Through the Lord's prompting, and an invitation from a good friend, that summer he went with a short-term team to Hungary, helping with a building project and a week-long youth programme put on by a church in a small village. Brandon saw God at work in many ways and, more than ten years later, is still good friends with the village pastor and his wife.

When he returned home, he found himself suddenly much more aware of the people around him who came from other countries. He loved going to events put on by the university for international students, something that had hardly interested him at all before. There he met Réka, the only student from Hungary in the whole programme. Even though she was not a Christian, she was very interested in Brandon's impressions of her country and all that he had experienced there.

Réka began coming to Bible studies and, eventually, she too put her trust in Christ. The next year, when she returned to Budapest, Brandon was able to put her in contact with some Christians he had met the previous summer.

Later, Brandon returned to Hungary on a two-year mission team based in Budapest. He and Réka started going to a neighbourhood church where they met some other young people and formed a Bible study group. As people grew in their faith, in their enthusiasm they began bringing more and more of their friends. Several became Christians, others had their faith confirmed and strengthened. The group got to know other Christians and began reaching out in creative ways. They took trips together to help with different ministries around the country.

Ten years later, Brandon and Réka are married and have a little daughter. The Bible study group no longer meets, but the friendships have remained. For many who were part of it, the time spent in that group proved to be a very formative stage in their lives, and quite a few are now in leadership roles in different churches and ministries. Brandon and Réka continued their studies in biology and have both earned postgraduate degrees. Brandon now teaches at a university in Budapest, where he is able to be a witness for Christ in many ways, not least by offering reasoned arguments as to why Christians should be involved in environmental issues. Both he and Réka have become increasingly involved in environmental projects in both Hungary and South Africa, where they find many opportunities to be salt and light in a very challenging field and context.

And all along the way, the little Baptist church that Brandon first joined after becoming a Christian has kept in touch, supporting them in prayer, encouragement, and, at times, financially. It isn't too much to say that through Brandon and Réka this church's view of and involvement in mission has been considerably expanded.

One part of a much bigger picture

Going on a short-term mission project is about much more than just what you can get done in a few weeks or months, as important as that may be. In fact, the only way to appreciate the real significance of short-term mission projects is to keep the big picture in mind. Even though Brandon could tell you some encouraging stories about his first trip to Hungary, it is when the project is set in a long-term perspective that we can best see how it contributed to lasting change.

As we have seen, a short-term project can go a significant way in helping to develop a Mission Lifestyle in the individual, sending church and receiving locality. Let us take a closer look at these benefits.

Benefits to the individual who serves

There are many ways in which a short-term mission project can help us to grow in our faith and enhance the effectiveness of our witness for Christ. The following list touches on only a few. See if you can think of more!

Broader horizons	Stepping out of our comfort zone and into unfamiliar territory broadens our perspective. We experience first-hand what life is like in another part of the world, with all the needs and opportunities that are specific to that place. We also see how God is at work there. This will enable us to pray in a more informed and engaged manner in the future.
Greater flexibility	Using our gifts and skills in a different context from that to which we are accustomed can be extremely challenging. We may feel quite clumsy at times, and out of our depth. But challenges like this help us to be more flexible and responsive, thereby refining our ability to serve well.
Personal development	Unfamiliar settings have the tendency to highlight our strengths and weaknesses in new ways, especially in relation to how we function under stress. Applying what we learn enhances the effectiveness of our witness in any context.
Teamwork	Short-term teams teach us much about the great potential of teamwork. They also are prime examples of how demanding teamwork can be.

Relationships	Many relationships started through short-term teams last a lifetime, even when distance and cultural differences are factors.
Cross-cultural awareness	By going to another part of the world and working in another culture we experience personally the challenge of communicating and serving cross-culturally. This helps us to be able to relate better to those who are serving in this way long term, and to pray more insightfully for them. It can also increase our awareness of people from other cultures who live around us, and improve our ability to understand and reach out to them.
Discerning or confirming God's leading	It has often been said that you can only steer a ship when it is moving. If you are seeking God's leading, get out and try some things! Whether you are confident that God wants you to serve long-term in your own country, or in another part of the world, among people of your own culture, or another, or even if you have little idea at all of how God wants you to serve, there are few steps you could take that would be helpful in clarifying or confirming his leading.

Why not take a few minutes right now to complete the 'Short-term Preferences Worksheet'. This is simply a tool to help you to begin to draw a profile of the type of project that would correspond to ministries that are on your heart, and to the particular skills and gifts you have to offer. It won't show you exactly what you should do, but it may help in narrowing down the options.

Short-Term Mission Preferences Worksheet

Who do you want to help?
People belonging to which ethnic groups?
People of which religions?
People in which socio-economic groups?
People in which regions, countries or cities?

Where do you want to serve?
In an urban or rural context?
In which particular regions?

What will you do?	Certain ✔	Possibly ✔	Unsure ✔
Outreach and evangelistic activities?			
Relief and development?			
Physical labour?			
Administration?			
Teaching?			
Music?			
Medical aid?			
Economic development?			
Pray?			

Who will you do this with?	Certain ✔	Possibly ✔	Unsure ✔
A team from my local church?			
A team from my place of study or work?			
A particular agency?			
People I already know on location?			
People I will get to know on location?			
With what? (Abilities and Recourses)	Certain ✔	Possibly ✔	Unsure ✔
I have the following skills:			
I have the following experience:			
I have the following resources:			
I could raise resources from:			
I have the following spiritual gifts:			
I want to do things I haven't done before.			

When will you go?	Certain ✔	Possibly ✔	Unsure ✔
Within the next 6 months			
Within the next year			
Within the next 2 years			
For how long will you go?	Certain ✔	Possibly ✔	Unsure ✔
My length of commitment is limited			
A few weeks			
3 months			
6 months			
1 year			
I want something with long-term options			

What preparation do you need?	✔
Training: *Orientation* *Language* *Specific skills*	
Legal: *Written will* *Power of attorney*	
Financial: *Out of debt* *Support raised* *System for transferring funds*	
Medical and health: *Examination* *Insurance* *Immunisations*	
Travel: *Tickets* *Visa* *Insurance* *Emergency arrangements*	

Support team: *Prayer* *Finances* *Communication* *Accountability and evaluation*	
Relational: Conflicts resolved *Satisfactory 'goodbyes'*	
(See the 'Code of Best Practice for Short-term Mission' at www.globalconnections.co.uk/code.asp)	

Use your answers as a guide to begin researching your options.

Benefits for the sending church

When God's people reach out to each other across vast distances, whether geographic or cultural, when we work together, shoulder to shoulder, united in the midst of tremendous diversity, then we begin to fulfil the visions seen repeatedly in Scripture of a vast throng from every nation giving honour to the King. Short-term, cross-cultural mission projects aren't the whole picture, but they certainly can be an important part of it. They are focused and practical. They take big theological concepts and turn them into the sweaty reality of hard work and fun.

Involvement on a short-term mission project can also be of tremendous benefit to the home or sending church of the individual. Julie was in her mid-teens when she went with a summer team to Jamaica. Her church, a comfortable but not too lively place, was aware she was going, but didn't seem overly interested. The leaders gave their OK, but many people couldn't even remember what country she was going to, or why. When she returned home, however, her stories of how she had seen God at work in the midst of tremendous need rattled her church to the core. It was as if she had awakened a slumbering athlete. Now her church is bursting with vision and is thoroughly involved in mission both at home and abroad. The church is developing a community Mission Lifestyle.

Not everyone's experience is as earth-shattering as Julie's but, none the less, by going on a short-term team there is great potential that God will use your involvement to bring about change at home. The possibilities are actually quite similar to those we looked at in the previous section:

Broader horizons, other perspectives – you may be surprised by how many people will be sincerely interested in hearing about your experience. Some might even want to stay in touch, if possible, during the brief time that you are away. You can be their eyes and ears, hands and feet. By sharing your experience, you can help to expand people's horizons a little more, even if they won't ever have the opportunity of going themselves. You can help people to see and appreciate other perspectives, which will in turn help them to understand and care for others in better ways.

Greater flexibility – the more your church is involved, the more it will become evident that things in other parts of the world don't always work the way we expect them to. This can be frustrating at times, but the lessons learnt can help us all to be more patient and understanding, even in our home context.

Ministry development – you might be able to introduce your church to some of the new, or at least different, ideas and methods that you will see during your trip. Sometimes a fresh idea from outside can make all the difference in church's ministry. A short-term trip can also be an encouragement as you begin to see that what God is doing in your home church is quite special and unique.

Teamwork

The best short-term teams are organised in such a way that there is direct communication between your church, those ministering at the location to which you go, and whatever agency (if any) is also involved. (See the 'Code of Best Practice for Short-term Mission' at www.globalconnections.co.uk/code.asp) This might be a stretching experience for your church, but everyone benefits when we learn

	more about how to function well in partnerships and teams.
Relationships	Short-term teams spark many 'sister-church' relationships. Even if no formal ties are made, personal relationships are often established, which greatly enrich the lives of those involved.
Cross-cultural awareness	Your experience can also help your church to be able to relate better to those who are serving cross-culturally long term and to pray more insightfully for them. It can help in the same way with respect to your church's relationship with people from other cultures.
Discerning or confirming God's leading	Julie's story is an excellent example of how God can use the short-term experience of a young girl to breathe new vision, energy and direction into a church.

How much the local church benefits from an individual's involvement will be influenced by a number of factors, including:

- How much of a global mission vision does the local church already have?
- Did the individual who went on a short-term project decide alone, or was the decision reached in consultation with the sending church leadership?
- What is the relationship between the individual and the church leadership? Is it one of mutual respect? Does the individual seek and value input? Does the individual

know and trust the church leadership? Does the leadership know and trust the individual?

• Were people in the church well informed about the project, and was there a sense of expectation? Was the
  individual able to form a 'support team'?

• Was the church excited about the individual going? Did
  people in the church feel as if the individual was repre-
  senting them?

• Did the individual keep the church well informed about
  his or her experiences while on the trip, and give the
  church a clear report upon return?

• Did he or she share what was learnt? (See the Short-term
  Mission Evaluation Worksheet)

• Did the church connect with the people the individual
  worked with on the trip?

• Have both the church and the individual talked about
  ideas as to how they could become further involved?

One last thought: don't be too disappointed if there is a
sense that many people in the sending church are not that
interested. For many, it will be very difficult to relate to
those who have been on a short-term project, sometimes
simply because they are so wrapped up in their own lives
and cares. Do not overdo it by pressuring them too much.
Instead, try to understand them. Keep patiently and
humbly sharing what God has been teaching and showing
you. And keep praying for them, that God will open their
eyes to what he wants to do through them in this world.

Benefits for the receiving church

Considering the incredible amount of effort that is needed
to host a short-term team, local workers might sometimes
be tempted to wonder whether the results are always
worth it. But here, once again, it is necessary to keep the

big picture in mind.

Whether the project is construction, relief distribution, a camp, a training seminar or an evangelistic outreach, extra manpower, specific expertise and added resources are usually welcome. But there are some difficult questions that must also be faced:

- How will a new building be maintained? Is it really appropriate in size and style for its purpose and context? Is it part of a sustainable plan?
- Does the relief effort express respect for the recipients and recognition of their dignity? Or does is simply create or reinforce dependency on others?
- How will the camps, seminars and outreaches be followed up?
- Do the short-termers have the necessary skills for the task at hand? Will they be able to overcome the language barrier at all? How long will it take to repair the damage caused by cultural blunders?

If the project is well planned and clearly a part of a long-term, sustainable vision, then whatever is accomplished during the short-term, whether much or little, can be viewed as a step in the right direction. It is the long-term vision that gives value to the short-term effort.

But if only a little is accomplished, can it still be said to be worth the effort? If we view ministry as a one-way street, sometimes we would have to say no, it's not worth the effort. But ministry is not only a one-way street. When we work together, we benefit mutually. Iron sharpens iron. In fact, the organisation I work with is encouraging all of our teams and partner churches to view short-term teams firstly as an opportunity to invest in the participants themselves and only secondly as a means of getting extra help for the work. When that part of the equation is embraced, then every short-term team, regardless of expertise, experience and resource, is worth the effort.

More than this, by hosting a short-term team, local people are able to benefit in the same ways that the team members themselves do, yet without going anywhere! They are faced with the same cross-cultural issues, the same differences in perspective, the same communication challenges, the same stretching beyond their comfort zone. Once again, iron sharpens iron, and interaction with people from another culture, from another part of the world, provides great opportunity for enriching our lives and ministry, if we approach it with good preparation and a healthy attitude.

Facing criticism

Not everyone thinks that short-term mission projects are such a great idea. At some point you will probably hear people say things like:

> That's not real mission! Where's the commitment, the willingness to devote your whole life to one group of people living in a remote and needy region?

> What can you accomplish in only a few weeks or months anyway, especially when you have little or no understanding of the culture and can't speak the language? Sounds more like spiritualised tourism to me.

> Shame! All that money spent just so that you can go and see how people live in another part of the world, take a few pictures, help out a little on building project maybe, and share your testimony through translation. Who knows if the translator even really translated what you said? And if he did, what kind of relevance does your story have for the people living there?

Short-term teams are more hassle than they are worth! They're just a distraction to satisfy the curiosity of some rich young people and let them feel like they've done something to help the world. Think of what could be accomplished if all the money spent on short-term teams were invested in worthwhile projects. Why go to the other side of the world when there is so much need right here?

Sure, it's true that through ineffectiveness, wasted resources and incredible insensitivity some short-term efforts have justly earned criticism. But often the criticism itself is short sighted, focused only on immediate, quantifiable results rather than on long-term developments. And even when there are at times valid concerns, it is irresponsible to then draw the conclusion that all such efforts are ill advised. Short-term projects can be done well and, when they are, they play an extremely important role in mission. When faced with such criticism, ask yourself whether it is a justified critique, or simply a failure to take a long-term, big-picture perspective.

Evaluate and learn

So that as many lessons are learnt as possible, keep a diary of the short-term trip that records thoughts and emotions as well as activities and what God is teaching.

You might also find the following exercise helpful to see commonalities and differences in culture.

Experiencing other cultures

When you go cross-culturally, you might find the following exercise helpful in beginning to identify the differences between your home culture and the one you have just entered. Those in the host culture might also find your answers helpful in making them aware of the culture you have come from. It's great too for helping to make new friends in the host culture.

Step 1

Answer the questions from your own cultural point of view. This is the 'Home' culture.

Step 2

Meet with someone from the culture you've now entered to ask him or her the same questions, filling in the answers in the 'Host Culture' column.

Question	Home Culture	Host Culture
Name people who are prominent in the following areas: Politics Religion The Arts		
Who are the country's national heroes and heroines?		
Can you sing or 'hum' the national anthem?		
What languages are spoken?		
What is the predominant religion? Is it a state religion? What are the sacred writings?		
What are the most important religious ceremonies and observances? How regularly do people participate in them?		
How do members of the predominant religion feel about other religions?		
What are the most common forms of marriage ceremonies and celebrations?		
What is the attitude towards divorce? Extra-marital relations? Plural marriage?		
What is the attitude towards gambling?		
What is the attitude towards drinking?		
Is the price asked for merchandise fixed or are customers expected to bargain? How is the bargaining conducted?		
If, as a customer, you touch or handle merchandise for sale, will the storekeeper think you are knowledgeable, inconsiderate, within your rights or completely outside your rights?		

How do people organise their daily activities? What is the normal meal schedule? Is there a daytime rest period? What is the customary time for visiting friends?		
What foods are most popular and how are they prepared?		
What things are taboo in this society?		
What is the usual dress for women? For men? Do teenagers wear jeans?		
Do hairdressers use similar techniques used in the 'home' culture? How much time do you need to allow for an appointment at the hairdressers?		
What are the special privileges of age or sex?		
If you are invited to dinner, should you arrive early, on time or late? If late, how late?		
On what occasions would you present or accept gifts from people in the country? What kind of gifts would you exchange?		
Do some flowers have a particular significance?		
How do people greet one another – shake hands, embrace?		
How do they leave one another?		
What are the important holidays and how is each observed?		
What are the favourite recreational activities for: Adults Teenagers Children		

What sports are popular?		
What kinds of TV programmes are shown? What social purposes do they serve?		
What is the wage of the average person and what are the living conditions of the average person like?		
What games do children play? Where do children congregate?		
How are children disciplined at home?		
Are children usually present at social occasions and ceremonies? If they are not, how are they cared for?		
What kind of public transport is available? Do all classes of people use it?		
Who has the right of way on the roads: vehicles, animals or pedestrians?		
Is military training compulsory?		
Are the largest circulation newspapers generally friendly towards: the home culture America UK Germany?		
What kinds of options do foreigners have in choosing a place to live?		
What kind of health service is available?		
Is education 'free'? Compulsory?		
In schools are children segregated by: sex Age Race Religion Class?		

How are the children disciplined in schools?		
Where are the important universities in the country? If university education is sought abroad, to what countries and universities do students go?		

The questions are my adaptation of an original publication found in - *Survival Kit for Overseas Living*, 4th ed. by Robert Kohls. Copyright 2001. ISBN 1-85788-292-X. It is reprinted and adapted here with permission of Intercultural Press Inc., Yarmouth ME, (USA).

*　　*　　*

Evaluating Your Experience

Upon your return, fill in the evaluation worksheet. It might be best to share your diary and evaluation sheet with your sending church or fellowship. That way, its members are involved in what you have done, and can see what lessons you have learnt as well as what lessons they can learn from your experience. Also, share your completed evaluation form with the agency you went with and the local situation you served in.

Evaluating takes time, and it is important to make time for yourself; those who supported you in your venture; and for those who you went to serve.

You might find the 'Code of Best Practice for Short-term Mission' helpful not only in your evaluation but also in the selection of a short-term project. This can be found at www.globalconnections.co.uk/code.asp. It was written by representatives from a wide spectrum of churches and organisations with extensive experience in short-term projects, with the aim of helping people avoid some of the common mistakes and pitfalls.

Short-Term Mission Evaluation Worksheet

After your mission trip, answer the following questions honestly and share your answers with your support team and church leadership. If appropriate you could also share it with the people you worked with on location and the agency you went with.

Briefly describe your trip stating dates, location and ministry undertaken.
In what ways were your expectations met?
How could you have been prepared better?
What positive surprises did you encounter?
What disappointments did you have to overcome?
List 5 major lessons learnt 1 2 3 4 5

In what ways did God use the trip to show you more about himself?

In what ways did God use the trip to show you more about yourself?

In what ways did God use the trip to show you more about others?

What new things did you experience or try?

If you were to repeat the trip, what improvements would you want to make?

In what ways did your involvement benefit:
Your local church

The people you served

Yourself

Do you think your involvement detrimental in anyway?

Would you consider your involvement an efficient and effective use of resources? Explain your answer.

Do you think that your life style and ministry activities were culturally appropriate?

What did you learn about this other culture?

What life lessons did you learn from the other culture?

Do you feel you were you prepared for your return home? Explain your answer.

How well did your Support Team fulfil its various responsibilities? Give details.

Look back at your responses in the 'Short-term Mission Preferences Worksheet' and assess how you have changed.

Have a go!

If you've never been on a short-term mission project, perhaps it's time for you to allow God to widen your horizons. Perhaps God wants to get you away for a while from all that is familiar and safe and let you taste first-hand what life and ministry in another part of the world is like. Perhaps he wants to use such an experience to show you more about how and where he wants you to serve long term. You would be surprised how many people can look back on a short-term mission trip as a turning point in their life. Talk with others about it, people who can give you wise advice. And talk with God about it: ask him what he wants.

Don't forget that your ongoing embracing of a Mission Lifestyle doesn't end when you return from your ministry trip. But be warned – many people who go on short-term mission trips get the (wonderful) shock of their lives when they discover that God really does want them to pull up their roots after all and move to a whole new culture and setting to bear long-term witness for him there. Greg came to Europe from Canada on a two-year commitment when he was nineteen. That was almost seventeen years ago!

Be warned – a short-term mission project will affect you profoundly. You'll listen to the news differently. You'll look at people differently. You'll communicate with God differently. Your faith will be stretched, as will your patience and your endurance. God refines his servants. Short-term teams aren't his only method, but they are of one of his very effective ones.